A COMPASSIONATE, MODERATE POLITICAL PLATFORM FOR 2024

A COMPASSIONATE, MODERATE POLITICAL PLATFORM FOR 2024

CHRISTOPHER EBBE, PH.D., ABPP

Copyright 2023 by Christopher Ebbe, Ph.D.
All rights reserved.
Christopher Ebbe, Ph.D.
14156 SW 115th Terrace
Dunnellon FL 34432

Printed in the USA
ISBN: 979-8-9888764-0-3

COSTS PAID FOR BY CAMPAIGN EBBEFORPRESIDENT

Cover and interior book design by Scribe Freelance
www.scribefreelance.com

CONTENTS

PREFACE..xiii

WHY AM I SEEKING TO BE PRESIDENT? AND WHO AM I? 3
   WHAT IS HAPPENING IN OUR COUNTRY?.......................................3
   WHY AM I RUNNING FOR PRESIDENT? 6
   THE ISSUES THAT I WILL FOCUS ON IF ELECTED 8
- restoring equality among citizens
- restoring amity and acceptance among citizens
- bringing truth to politics
- diminishing the power of the two major political parties
- establishing compromise as the norm in our democracy
- reforming our tax system and attitudes
- making elections about who can do the job best
- jobs for all and a wage for a decent life
- encouraging civil discourse on political issues among citizens
- revising our immigration policy
- encouraging better emotional health for citizens

   THE KIND OF SOCIETY THAT MY PLATFORM WILL PRODUCE 10
   DOES MY CANDIDACY HAVE A CHANCE?.......................................12
   WHO AM I? 13

FUNDAMENTAL PRINCIPLES OF GOOD GOVERNMENT 17
   BASIC HUMAN PSYCHOLOGICAL NEEDS....................................... 17
   EQUALITY... 18
   RESPECT 18
   STATUS 18
   HOW DEMOCRATIC GOVERNMENT CAN FUNCTION BEST 20

THE PRESIDENCY—THE REALITY (OR UNREALITY) OF
   PRESIDENTIAL POWER.. 22
HONESTY 23
RESPONSIBLITY 24
FAIRNESS 24
INTEGRITY 25
SERVING THE CITIZENS IS MORE IMPORTANT THAN
   GETTING ELECTED.. 26
SERVING ALL CITIZENS AND NOT ONLY ONE'S SUPPORTERS 28
GOVERNMENT BY PRINCIPLES RATHER THAN CABAL 29
AN INFORMED CITIZENRY—VOTER EDUCATION 30
FIGHTING VS. COMPROMISE..31
COMPETITION 31
ALLIANCES AND VOTE TRADING... 32
WORKING TOGETHER 33
NATIONAL SERVICE 33
IS DEMOCRACY REALLY WHAT WE WANT? 34

AMITY AND ACCEPTANCE AMONG CITIZENS................37
CARING FOR OTHERS 38
   Feeling Positively Toward Others... 40
   Feeling Warmly Toward Others... 42
   Seeing Ourselves As Basic Equals With Others 42
   Wanting Good Things For Others... 44
   Giving Others Basic Acceptance 46
OVERCOMING BARRIERS TO CARING.. 48
   Ignorance and Fear of Others.. 48
   Past Disappointments 48
   Feeling Unlovable Ourselves... 48
   Anger About Not Being Cared About 49
   Dislike For Others... 49
   Seeing Others As Enemies 49
DEVELOPING CARING ABILITIES 53
EXPANDING OUR CIRCLE OF CARING.. 53

SPECIFIC POPULATIONS 55
The Position of the Marginalized and Disadvantaged 55
The Position of Women 56
#MeToo 57
The Position of Men 58
The Other (Another Side) 59
The Position of Children 59
The Position of Non-Gender-Conforming Citizens 60

ENCOURAGING TRUTH IN GOVERNMENT 63
HONESTY 64
POLITICAL SPEECH 65
LYING BY CANDIDATES AND ELECTED OFFICIALS 66
SOCIAL MEDIA 67

OUR TWO-PARTY SYSTEM 69

ACCEPTING COMPROMISE AS THE NORM FOR OUR DEMOCRACY 73
LIVING WITH COMPROMISE 75

TAXES, A BALANCED BUDGET, GOVERNMENT BORROWING, AND THE NATIONAL DEBT 77
TAXES 77
A BALANCED BUDGET, BORROWING, AND THE NATIONAL DEBT 80

MAKING ELECTIONS ABOUT WHO CAN DO THE JOB BEST 83
CHOOSING A PRESIDENT 83
JOB TASKS OF THE PRESIDENT 84
HOW DO I MATCH UP? 86

JOBS FOR ALL AND WAGES FOR A DECENT LIFE 91
JOBS FOR ALL 91
WAGES FOR A DECENT LIFE 95
WELFARE 98

HAVING CIVIL DISCOURSE ON SENSITIVE TOPICS 99
    DISCUSSING POLITICS WISELY AND COMPASSIONATELY 100

IMMIGRATION 109
    "THE WALL" 112

OTHER ISSUES INVOLVING GOVERNMENT 113
    FREE SPEECH 113
    PRIVACY 114
    CLIMATE CHANGE AND OTHER GLOBAL PROBLEMS 115
        Fossil Fuels 116
    POPULATION 117
    INFRASTRUCTURE 119
    SOCIAL SECURITY 119
    FINANCIAL ACCOUNTABILITY 120
    PORK 121
    MERIT HIRING (NO SPOILS) 121
    SUPREME COURT 122
    UNRELATED AMENDMENTS TO BILLS IN CONGRESS 123
    UP OR DOWN VOTES ON ALL BILLS 124
    BIG STATES VS. SMALL STATES 124
    FEDERAL VS. STATES 125
    UNFUNDED MANDATES 126
    OFFICIAL LANGUAGE 127
    A CONSTITUTIONAL CONVENTION 127

ELECTION ISSUES 129
    MY APPROACH TO ELECTIONS 129
    MOTIVES OF CANDIDATES 130
    TERM LIMITS 131
    COUNTING VOTES 131
    GERRYMANDERING 132
    MAKING IT HARD OR EASY TO VOTE 133
    CAMPAIGNS 133

ELECTORAL COSTS	134
PRESIDENT TRUMP	135

FOREIGN RELATIONS AND FOREIGN POLICY ... 137
WORLD PEACE	137
BEING NUMBER ONE	138
WORKING WITH OTHER COUNTRIES	139
NATO	140
THIRD WORLD DEVELOPMENT	141
RUSSIA	141
UKRAINE	142
CHINA	143
ISRAEL	143
TAIWAN	144
AFGHANISTAN	145
INTERFERENCE BY FOREIGN GOVERNMENTS: THE "RUSSIA INVESTIGATION"	146
SEEING THINGS FROM THE POINT OF VIEW OF OTHER COUNTRIES	147
WARS	148
GOVERNMENT SECRECY/COVERT OPERATIONS	150

HEALTH CARE ... 153
MEDICAL CARE	153
COVID	154
ASSISTED SUICIDE	155
ABORTION	156
DRUGS	157
POLLUTION	159
HOMELESSNESS	160
REFERENDA	162

PSYCHOLOGICAL FUNCTIONING AND HEALTH ... 163

x   A COMPASSIONATE, MODERATE POLITICAL PLATFORM FOR 2024

NATIONAL DEFENSE (Including Non-Military National Defense) 169

JUSTICE SYSTEM ISSUES 171
    LAW AND ORDER 171
    PUNISHMENT OR REHABILITATION? 172
    BAIL AND A SPEEDY TRIAL 173
    THE DEATH PENALTY 174
    OUR ADVERSARIAL SYSTEM 175
    GUNS AND MASS SHOOTINGS 175
    POLICE BRUTALITY 177

THE ECONOMY 181
    GLOBALIZATION OF THE ECONOMY 181
    INCOME INEQUALITY 182
    CAPITALISM 183
    JOBS FOR ALL AND WAGES FOR A DECENT LIFE 184
    UNIONS 184
    PRIVATIZING/CONTRACTING OUT 185
    SOCIALISM 186

EDUCATION 189
    EDUCATION 189
    EQUAL EDUCATION FOR ALL 192
    NEWS AND ENTERTAINMENT MEDIA AS EDUCATION SOURCES 192
    STUDENT DEBT 194

RACE AND IDENTITY 197
    DIVERSITY AND DIFFERENCE 197
    RACIAL/ETHNIC CONFLICT 198
    BLACK LIVES MATTER 198
    IDENTITY POLITICS 199
    AFFIRMATIVE ACTION 199
    "WOKENESS" AND CANCEL CULTURE 200

RELIGION 203
   RELIGION AND PUBLIC LIFE 203
   WHAT I BELIEVE 205
   WHAT WOULD JESUS DO? 206

A VERY BRIEF SUMMARY OF MY PRIORITIES 207

FINAL WORD 211

BIBLIOGRAPHY 213

APPENDIX A 215

INDEX 219

PREFACE

I am writing this book to inform the voting public about my priorities if I were elected President in 2024 and the principles on which I would operate as President. Those priorities are—

- restoring equality among citizens
  We are so divided along economic and class lines that the value of the individual citizen has been degraded. We are all equal as citizens, and we are all of equal value to the nation. The primacy of citizen voices for politics has to be restored. I will develop programs for constant, organized feedback from citizens to government, including annual referenda on such things as how much should be spent on healthcare, and I will give you weekly, specific feedback on how your government is progressing.
- restoring amity and acceptance among citizens
  Our divisions have been magnified until we perceive those who are different as enemies. We must learn to be more comfortable with difference, through greater understanding of others' beliefs and needs. We should also care more about each other's welfare, through developing greater empathy and recognizing our similarities. We are all Americans, all in the same boat, and we must work together to benefit all Americans, rather than trying to get more for ourselves and "win" by making others live as we think they should.
- bringing truth to politics
  There is such a thing as truth, even in this post-modern, post-facts environment, and it is our duty as citizens to seek to understand our situation and issues as well as we can, so that we can elect the right people. Otherwise, we will be completely at the mercy of those who seek personal power. I will always tell you the truth about what is going on, including who in government is keeping us from making necessary progress.

- diminishing the power of the two major political parties
  Having two behemoth parties has suppressed political discussion in the legislative process, since the parties funnel all discussion of their members into only two final positions. This eliminates much of our potential creativity in solving problems, and voting by party gives us a skewed picture of what our Congresspersons and Senators actually think. Congress needs our individual input, and Congresspersons should vote what individually they actually believe rather than how the party tells them to vote.
- establishing compromise as the norm for our democracy
  Democracy is ideally a system of gathering the equally valuable input from all citizens and then fashioning the best solutions possible at the moment for each and every problem. Democracy should not be about who can "win" and force everyone else to do as they direct; it must be about making the best compromises possible on every issue. The current emphasis on winning make us enemies unnecessarily. I will work for effective and acceptable compromises for all of our problems (which will mean that some citizens will have to give up their crusades to force their moral beliefs and attitudes on everyone else!).
- reforming our tax system and attitude
  Taxes should be based on how much Congress appropriates each year, because that should be the amount of taxes collected *in the following year*. This will cure the deficit problem, eliminate government borrowing, and show you exactly what your representatives have voted for. Taxes are to pay for what we together decide to do as a country, and if citizens don't like the amount of their taxes, then paying the next year for the previous year's appropriation will lead immediately to electing new persons to Congress. Taxes are not something to be avoided, and we should not idolize those who do best at avoiding paying their share.
- making elections about who can do the job best
  The job of President is too important to be a popularity contest. We should always elect the person who is best qualified to actually do the job. (See my analysis of the job of President and the skills required, below and at www.livewiselydeeply.com *under "government/politics" and then "presidential choice."*)
- jobs for all and wages for a decent life
  We have a large proportion of jobs that do not pay enough to live on. To address this, we should get more people working (through public support if not by our businesses), and all jobs should pay

enough to have a "decent life" (through shared support by our taxes and our businesses).
- encouraging civil discourse on political issues among citizens
  It is not difficult to understand how to have useful, civil discussions about difficult issues, though it may be difficult to actually implement the steps required (basically seeking to understand others' views and share your own, without seeking to convert the other person). I will exemplify this approach in my interactions with Congress and with all citizens.
- encouraging better emotional health for citizens
  The principles of good emotional health are not difficult to understand (basically, seeking to be happy through having adequate self-worth and an adequate sense of security, while valuing and not harming others). I will promote programs that support citizens' self-worth and security, and I will help society to help especially those who could end up trying mass shootings of their fellow citizens!
- updating our immigration laws
  We must revise our definition of asylum, determine a fair way to triage those who are likely to fit our definition at the border using beefed up hearing and detention facilities (and many more hearing judges), deport those not likely to qualify for asylum (to gather more information themselves, and continue accepting non-asylum/non-refugee immigrants as we do now, to maintain the workforce that we need.

Since our elected representatives are so far away and isolated from us, and since many hope to be career politicians, it has become accepted that for their own best interests they should let us voters know as little about themselves as possible. The belief is that voters are more likely to pick up on a trait or issue that they see as negative (and then not vote for the candidate) than they are a positive trait or issue.

My belief (and hope) is that many voters are smarter than this and wish to understand the issues and candidates, and I hope that in their minds, disclosure will be seen as a positive. Just as important, I believe that candidates should seek office primarily to serve our citizens and our country (rather than primarily for their own careers). I want the best qualified person to win, and voters will not know who the best qualified is unless we have more disclosure by candidates than we have had recently. I do not believe that candidates should "fight" to win elections but should offer themselves and information about themselves so that the voters can make a good decision. In the chapter on electing a President you will find an analysis of the skills and abilities it takes to function well as a President, as well as some assessment of where I might stand in terms of those skills and abilities.

In the body of the book you will find my positions on all of the issues I could think of to include, including the priorities above, plus abortion, climate change, the role of religion in our democracy, competing with China, the current status of our disadvantaged and marginalized groups, etc. Probably the most important issue currently is how we can work together (instead of fighting each other) to make this the best country we can make it. All it would take is adopting the attitude that each citizen deserves the same consideration from government as every other citizen and should be treated with respect and courtesy by us all, all the time. No winners or losers, just equality. This attitude will set us up to interact in useful ways instead of trying to impose our own views on each other. *Understanding each other's needs* and *effective compromise* are our key tools in working together.

My priorities are described in detail, and opposing views are noted briefly for each issue. Using the extensive Table of Contents, you can readily locate those issues that are most important to you. At the end there is a from that you could use to compare candidates before voting.

My candidacy is no doubt quixotic, but I am raising issues that could really change our politics. If you like what you see here, please let your friends, relatives, and neighbors know about me, so they can see for themselves the ideas I am offering! I will have a website in early Sept., 2023 (www.ebbeforpresident.com) with blog and issue videos.

A COMPASSIONATE, MODERATE POLITICAL PLATFORM FOR 2024

In the melee of our presidential elections, citizens get little in-depth information about what candidates are committed to and what they would do if elected, instead being targeted with sound bites, slogans, disinformation, and outright lies. This document gives information about what I would do and how I would function as President and is an example of what might be useful for voters to have in order to learn about all candidates and select the right one. I am a political moderate and registered as an Independent voter (rather than a Democrat or a Republican). I will represent *everyone* equally, without special considerations for Progressives or for MAGA Republicans. Since one of my recommendations for improving our ability to cope with the country's problems is to get to the truth and to find best compromises by explaining the other side of things as well as speaking in favor or one's own positions, contrasts with other opinions are included for each section (in the print book). Bear in mind that these are my opinions as of the current date (6-23), and they may change as new information becomes available.

WHY AM I SEEKING TO BE PRESIDENT? AND WHO AM I?

WHAT IS HAPPENING IN OUR COUNTRY?

Our nation is going through a period of conflict and unhappiness, resulting largely from economic globalization, growing wealth inequality, and increased exposure to more of our fellow citizens through the internet.

The rest of the world is catching up to us economically, partly through globalization of business and trade which has led to greater specialization in products produced and a resulting loss of jobs here related to the products that are now more cheaply produced in other countries. This trend toward equalization of wealth among countries is almost inevitable if we have a global economy, as the wealthier nations have already used most of their ideas about growth and don't work quite as hard at it as they used to, and the less wealthy nations imitate the more wealthy nations' approaches and work harder to get what the more wealthy have. It will take several decades more for labor costs to equalize around the world.

On average our citizens are doing better economically, but this is an average of both more rich people, more poor people, and many failing to progress in our country, and many believe that there is now no way for them to rise in society, since wealth controls so much opportunity, and the wealthy have so much power and so many advantages. As a result, more people are disheartened and angry about the fading of the "American dream," which has led to more protests and more riots, and has enhanced the "sovereignty movement" ("my property is a sovereign state, and your laws don't apply here") and the formation of groups with intent to harm the nation (including local militias). Businesses have responded to global competition by reducing benefits, slashing retirement plans, and forgetting any sense of loyalty to workers, which leaves workers feeling abandoned, angry, and hopeless.

While we have lost manufacturing jobs, we now have many more jobs related to information technology and automation (more white collar jobs), but unfortunately those without jobs are not capable of performing these new jobs, and automation aims directly at reducing the number of manufacturing jobs even further. The supposedly crucial nimbleness of businesses in a global economy results in moving jobs around much more, for even marginally lower costs, and citizens, who are by and large emotionally attached to their hometowns, are reluctant to be always moving to keep up with the job movements.

With the even greater spread of income and wealth, those toward the lower end are made to feel even worse about themselves, which threatens are basic democratic assumptions about the basic equality of all citizens and causes some people to seek a powerful leader who can turn back the clock or "take from the rich and give to the poor." Capitalism leads inevitably to more wealth at the top, and we have not adjusted to this (e.g, by increasing taxes on the rich) to preserve our sense of all being "in the same boat" and all being equally politically. There has been remarkably little violence over these economic changes so far, but more will come if we do not give citizens at the lower end of the economic spectrum more hope for the future.

As society has become more complex (supposedly to solve more problems), more things are being taken care of by specialists, and people have naturally felt less secure in general (since we now have to trust others whom we do not know). We have turned over our survival to others (much more than we did a hundred years ago) and would not know how to survive at our current level if left to our own devices. Average people have no knowledge about how to build a house or run a power plant, manufacture plastics, create medicines, program cell phones, or grow crops. Our greater insecurity stems from knowing that we couldn't maintain our lives on our own and knowing that since these things are being done by other human beings, mistakes will be made which will affect us (viz., the Texas winter power issues of two years ago). Also, greater complexity has created more opportunities for criminality (the internet, greater anonymity). This has led to greater need for monitoring the behavior of everyone (like red-light cameras and drones) so that we can catch criminals, but this intrudes on our "privacy," and we feel less secure since our own peccadillos and lawbreaking will now be seen and our behavior may be misinterpreted. Since we believe in rugged individualism, we care not for the needs of fellow citizens and see the only solution to lawbreaking to be greater punishment, rather than efforts to give lawbreakers opportunity to shift their values and join productive society while in prison.

People in our country are less happy now than they used to be (see the World Happiness Project), since many people feel more stress about keeping their jobs and less hope about their futures. Americans are working more hours than Europeans for roughly the same quality of life that Europeans have, with the gains from this going largely to our wealthier citizens. The information revolution has made many workers vulnerable to being used during their off-time by bosses who can and feel free to contact them at home and on vacation. Employees comply out of fear of losing their job.

Greater exposure to the views of others through the internet has led to more open and visible "culture war," so that many citizens now fear other citizens or see them as enemies and not just people with whom they have differences. The warlike nature of these expressions on all sides demonstrates one of my main concerns—that we in this country don't know how to understand each other or to find best compromises for our joint problems. We are all aiming at "winning" and forcing the other side to live as we think everyone should live. This is anti-democratic, as two of the bedrock principles of a democracy are that the voices of each and every one of us are essentially equal in weight in government and that as long as we are not harming others, we have freedom to live as we want. Differences should lead to informative discussion (to ensure that there is a minimum of ignorance and to acquaint everyone with the creative ideas on all sides) and then to seeking the best possible compromise for the current time (which could become the rule or law on the matter). We need leadership and education toward making these principles (equal weight and compromise) the universally understood way to solve problems.

A number of well-meaning citizens have focused on enhancing the self-esteem of minorities and disadvantaged groups by lauding their status(s)—being Black, being female, being an immigrant, being "queer," etc. This has become known as "identity politics," although the basic issue (how people feel about themselves) is not political. Seeing this praise for these groups, other citizens have reacted angrily (or with hurt feelings actually) because they feel that this pushes *them* down the status ladder even further. We should all be able to feel good about ourselves, and some people and groups need more help with this than others, but emphasizing differences – even as value points—also creates more division among the citizenry. I believe that we would do better to focus on everyone feeling better (Blacks, Hispanics, immigrants, women, Christian Nationalists, Proud Boys, and everyone else). Equality is the answer—not fighting for status.

We have trained our citizens to feel good mostly about consuming (*having* more), so they don't know how to be satisfied with what they have (which in most cases is more than most other people around the world have), and they also don't know how to decide for themselves what is enough. They don't know how to actively entertain themselves (by greater participation in group activities and perhaps even by reading and thinking!), because distraction and fantasy feel-goods fill up our lives under the more acceptable title of "entertainment" and cause us to withdraw personally from singing, dancing, sports, etc., since we would not be "good enough" compared to the best.

Changes in our economy together with our very human drive to eliminate pain and discomfort whenever possible has led to drug and alcohol abuse and medication misuse sufficient to cause dysfunction and even death for too many (which is also one indication that we have a lot of unhappy and hopeless people in our country).

The internet has provided vastly increased opportunities for communication, but it has also exposed our penchant for lying and seeing only our own viewpoints, as well as the sorry self-esteem of so many, which they try to improve through collecting "likes" as well as attacking and competing with others or presenting false identities on social media. My platform will also begin to address some of these attitudinal issues!

WHY AM I RUNNING FOR PRESIDENT?

I am moved to offer myself as a candidate for President partly to bring back into public focus the value and purpose of democracy and its principles (equality and compromise) and to use this focus to induce everyone to work together more rather than spend so much energy and vitriol in conflicts over power. We have forgotten much of what we share while we fight over who has power. I do not believe that any group should have the power to force other people to live as the group with the power wants everyone to live unless there are compromises (agreements) that become law. Instead, our joint decisions should reflect what can be done for all groups at the same time, through understanding each other and finding the most effective compromises possible.

I am also moved to serve as President by my empathy for those in our society who have difficult lives or are chronically unhappy unnecessarily (in my opinion), and I believe that a huge proportion of our citizens get by OK but are not really happy, even if they do not identify themselves as having a problem (uninspiring jobs, lack of opportunity, boredom with restrictive roles, etc.). We can do better, by taking better care of ourselves and nurturing caring relationships with others.

I am calling myself "a compassionate president" (if elected, of course) as something that distinguishes me from other candidates. Compassion is being aware of the suffering of others and wishing for that suffering to be lessened. I am very aware of the suffering of our middle class and working class citizens, due to globalization and our increasing wealth inequity, and I am determined to do something about these things, through people understanding each other better and learning the value of compromise. I care about how Americans feel about themselves and about their fellow citizens. I am also aware of the suffering caused by our culture wars and political power struggles, and I wish very much to reduce that suffering and conflict. Acting on my sense of compassion, I will treat everyone as equals, with respect and courtesy, irrespective of status in our society. This also means that I will not rant and rave about anyone or any group or insult them, even when I speak out about behavior that is adding to our collective suffering.

Wanting to reduce unnecessary suffering through improving how we relate to each other and how we take care of each other is my only motive for seeking the presidency. I'm not interested in power or glory (though I must admit I do like recognition). I assume that many of our elected representative are aware, also, or somewhat aware of this suffering, but they seem to treat it as something that no one can change or that can be changed only by one side or the other "winning," and I disagree wholeheartedly with this. I know that something can be done, if our citizens and representatives are willing.

As I believe that we always choose actions that are in our own best interest (since doing things that are in the best interest of others is often in our own best interest as well), seeking the presidency will be in my interest because I feel good when I can help others and help others to feel good, and secondly because I would prefer to live in a country in which people cooperated with each more cheerfully and cared about each other more, which I will promote to the best of my ability as President. I do not seek or enjoy power over others, though I would like to influence people to see that what I propose will be beneficial. Noting that power is often corrupting, I will seek daily to examine whether I am sticking to my claim of not wanting power over others!

I would be 81 when taking office, if elected, which does not seem to be a necessary deterrent from serving, since Mr. Trump and Mr. Biden are both approximately that age, too! My health is excellent, and I take a brisk walk for 30 minutes every day. I will make my medical records completely open to the public if necessary—something that I'm pretty sure neither Mr. Trump nor Mr. Biden would do. I would not run for a second term, which is both prudent from a health perspective and a gift in that it would enable me to act in the best interest of the country without worrying about re-election.

THE ISSUES THAT I WILL FOCUS ON IF ELECTED

- restoring equality among citizens
  We are so divided along economic and class lines that the value of the individual citizen has been degraded. We are all equal as citizens, and we are all of equal value to the nation. The primacy of citizen voices for politics has to be restored. I will develop programs for constant, organized feedback from citizens to government, including annual referenda on such things as how much should be spent on healthcare. The Congress is supposed to be our link between citizens and government, but Congress has gotten so focused on the power struggle between parties that we citizens never know what they actually think or how they are conducting our business.
- restoring amity and acceptance among citizens
  Our divisions have been magnified until we perceive those who are different as enemies. We must learn to be more comfortable with difference, through greater understanding of others' beliefs and needs. We should also care more about each other's welfare, through developing greater empathy and recognizing our similarities. We are all Americans, in the same boat, and we must work together to benefit all Americans, rather than trying to get more for ourselves and "win" by making others live as we think they should.
- encouraging truth in politics
  There is such a thing as truth, even in this post-modern, post-facts environment, and it is our duty as citizens to seek to understand our situation and issues as well as we can, so that we can elect the right people. Otherwise, we will be completely at the mercy of those who seek personal power. I will always tell you the truth about what is going on, including who in government is keeping us from making necessary progress.
- diminishing the power of the two major political parties
  Having two behemoth parties has suppressed political discussion in the legislative process, since the parties funnel all discussion

of their members into only two final positions. This eliminates much of our potential creativity in solving problems, and voting by party gives us a skewed picture of what our Congresspersons and Senators actually think. Congress needs our individual input, and Congresspersons should vote what individually they actually believe rather than how the party tells them to vote.

- establishing compromise as the norm for our democracy
  Democracy is ideally a system of gathering the equally valuable input from all citizens and then fashioning the best solutions possible at the moment for each and every problem. Democracy should not be about who can "win" and force everyone else to do as they direct; it must be about making the best compromises possible on every issue. The current emphasis on winning leads to the parties putting off even voting on needed proposals if they cannot win at that moment, which leads to ineffective and then erratic government as they overturn previous "wins" by the other side. I will work for effective and acceptable compromises for all of our problems. This will mean some citizens will have to give up their crusades to force their moral beliefs and attitudes on everyone else!
- reforming our tax system and attitudes
  Taxes should be based each year on how much Congress appropriated the previous year, because we should "pay as we go" rather than increasing the national debt. This will cure the deficit problem. Taxes are to pay for what we together decide to do as a country, and if citizens don't like the amount of their taxes, then paying the next year for the previous year's appropriation will lead immediately to electing new persons to Congress. Taxes are not something to be avoided, and we should not idolize those who do best at avoiding paying their share.
- making elections about who can do the job best
  The job of President is too important to be a popularity contest. We should always elect the person who is best qualified to actually do the job. (See my analysis of the job of President and the skills required, below on this website and at www.livewiselydeeply.com\presidentialchoice.)
- jobs for all and wages for a decent life
  We have a large proportion of jobs that do not pay enough to live on. To address this, we should get more people working (by public support if not by our businesses), and all jobs should pay enough to have a "decent life" (through shared support by our taxes and our businesses).

- encouraging civil discourse on political issues among citizens
  It is not difficult to understand how to have useful, civil discussions about difficult issues, though it may be difficult to actually implement the steps required (basically seeking to understand others' views and share you own, without seeking to convert the other person to your point of view). I will exemplify this approach in my interactions with Congress and with all citizens.
- encouraging better emotional health for citizens
  The principles of good emotional health are not difficult to understand (basically, seeking to be happy through our productive actions, having adequate self-worth, and having an adequate sense of security, while valuing and not harming others. We have not prepared our children well for coping with the complex world we have created, and I will make public information and methods available for doing a better job of childrearing and of getting along with each other as equal citizens!
- revising our immigration policy
  The treatment of immigrants at our southern border, including our unwillingness to pay for staffing and other resources adequate to do any better, is a national disgrace. Only by having an up-to-date immigration law (which Congress refuses to attempt) can we do any better. I will press for a new law and for the money to do the job right.

THE KIND OF SOCIETY THAT MY PLATFORM WILL PRODUCE

Every principle and goal will have outcomes if implemented, including what kind of society it will produce. If our citizens are more intelligent, it will make our society more intelligent overall, and if our citizens are more compassionate, our overall society will have less internal conflict. You should know what my set of values and policies is likely to produce (and other candidates and parties should tell you what kind of country they will produce).

I would like for all of us to feel more secure and more valuable, and I would like to see our society be more tolerant, more accepting, more cooperative, and more compassionate (care for others more). I believe that this can be achieved if citizens are more knowledgeable about psychological, economic, and political realities and if they feel more responsible for their fellow citizens than they do now. My policies will aim to move society in this direction.

If you prefer to keep our current traditions of individualism (taking care only of number one) and fighting others for what you individually want, then you will probably not vote for me, but you should realize that you will then keep all the problems we have in human relations just as they are (crime, greed, corruption, contempt for others). You can't have it both ways. Realize, too, that if you want the more individually-oriented system, then there will be fewer safety nets for you when *you* have a problem. (This was glaringly obvious during the coronavirus crisis, where the government had to scramble to find ways to give money to citizens because we have no structure for doing so. We don't even have a list of all citizens.) Many aspects of developing ourselves as individuals are valuable, but this must include a strong sense of responsibility for ourselves and a compassionate concern for others.

People who vote for me will be those who value honesty and integrity and who want everyone to feel equal and equally valued in our society. They will want government to look out for all citizens and to always seek an acceptable balance of wealth and opportunity between all classes in society, even while encouraging creativity and hard work among all citizens.

I would like to see every citizen feel safe and valued, and I would like to see every citizen be satisfied with feeling safe and valued, without feeling that he/she must or should strive for more. Clearly it is striving to be "better than" others that creates so much of our interpersonal and internal problems. This striving to be "better than" others involves envy, jealousy, and hatred and results in much harm of persons by other persons. So much intrigue, joining together to look down on others, gossip, and nastiness could be reduced if we could be satisfied with feeling safe and valued for being ourselves, not for our position on the status hierarchy.

Be happy with being loved and safe. You don't have to "be" any more than that. Taking good care of yourself and your loved ones, raising capable and responsible children, and participating in government through voting knowledgeably and communicating with your representatives are more than enough to feel as if you have had a successful life. If feeling safe requires raising the financial level of some of our citizens, then we should get busy figuring out how to do that. As long as some people look down on others, for financial status or anything else, then those who are looked down on will resent it and will strive to equalize the situation or surpass those who looked down on them. The "trickle down" assumption about improving society financially will not work, as long as those higher on the hierarchy look down on anyone else.

I hereby issue a direct challenge to both Democrats and Republicans—if you have a vision of how you would like our society to be, then show us! I don't think they can do it, because our two largest parties are diverse enough that they won't be able to settle on a vision, and this fact—that they don't have a clear vision—is impeding our progress as a society, since they both claim that they should be in charge of that progress!

Other Opinions

Some people with opposing views think that only fear and force can induce people to act properly, and they believe that only if people are suffering will they seek something better (so the experience of poverty should be enough by itself to make people strive for something better). They believe that the motives of fear, envy, competition, and jealousy are good for society since they drive people to work harder. They think that love is nice but weak and unlikely to inspire people to be better. (Their emphasis on personal responsibility is appropriate, but ignoring the complexity of "making it" in our society today is unhelpful.)

DOES MY CANDIDACY HAVE A CHANCE?

It might appear at first that my candidacy, based on this platform and my actual characteristics (thoughtful, quiet, calm, reasonable, friendly, articulate, trustworthy, honest, looking for the best in people) could not possibly succeed. There's no flash, no anger or fear-mongering, no celebrity to offer. Also, on the money front, I have no personal resources for this task and will need financial support from voters (or from a billionaire). In my campaign, my major thrust will be to alert citizens to the realities of our plight. Right now we are *choosing* to fight rather than solve problems. We are forgetting about the common man. We need a return to paying attention to what the total public wants rather than what will get people re-elected. We should stop pitting some groups in society against others for the purpose of getting votes. And, we should challenge all politicians to solve problems, compromising when needed, rather than hold out until they can "win." If funding is sufficient, I will focus on informing the public about our problems and the potential changes in attitude needed, instead of trying to present a façade of myself that might inspire voters to vote for me. I personally have no fortune to spend on a campaign, which these days makes me different from most politicians! I can't by myself even pay for a publicist to help start getting the word out, so I'll be using Twitter and Facebook and my own website (www.ebbeforpresident.com) to communicate.

On the voting front, though, I sincerely believe that there are enough voters across the country who want a candidate that they can reasonably trust, who is smart, who will push for greater equality and more valuing of every citizen (rather than demeaning some to make others feel better), and who will press Congress to let go of their petty fighting for power and make the necessary compromises to do the best we can to solve our problems. I believe that there are enough voters to elect such a candidate, and right now, I seem to be the only candidate who fits that bill. (See the section on the job qualifications needed by a President.) If you know a potentially interested billionaire, suggest my name to him or her!

Whenever there are candidates who are neither Republican or Democrat, you may wonder why you should "waste your vote" by voting for someone who has "no chance of winning." We are at a point that we desperately need to get away from the two-party struggle for power, and I truly believe that there are enough voters who see this as important to actually sway an election. (Remember that only thirty percent of registered voters are Republicans and thirty percent Democrats.) Even if this is not enough voters to elect me, by voting for me you could be one of a sizeable enough group of voters in this election to convince the two major parties to get their act together and begin to serve all groups in our society by finding appropriate compromises.

If I do have something we could call a campaign (Twitter, Facebook, my own presidential website), I will focus on raising the above issues with the public. I would obviously need some sort of grassroots activity in order to spread the word to those who don't get information through the internet, and these would have to be volunteers inspired sufficiently by the importance of the stated issues. Volunteer help also would be needed to do whatever each state requires for a person to "get on the ballot." Otherwise I could be the only person ever elected President as a write-in!

WHO AM I?

I was born during World War Two, to parents who were traveling to various locations around the U.S. to build airfields for the government. I had a serious burn accident as a toddler but survived to enjoy some early years with our milk-goats on a lake near Kansas City. We moved to the small town of Trenton MO when I was four, where my father headed up a small construction company, and I was there until leaving for college. We had the typical small-town atmosphere—a county fair, a lazy river, football homecoming, Boy Scouts, ice skating on the pond in the winter, marching in the school band. Church participation (the Disciples of Christ) was very important for forming my character and defining my values.

I was lucky enough to get into the Massachusetts Institute of Technology, where I got a good and very stimulating education, though I changed from engineering as a goal to psychology and took as many philosophy and religion courses as I could at M.I.T. before graduating in 1965, after which I got married and started psychology graduate school at the Univ. of Missouri at Columbia.

I was drafted during graduate school (for Vietnam) but managed to switch from the Army to the Air Force where I could serve as a masters-level psychologist. After three years working at Wilford Hall USAF Hospital in San Antonio, the Air Force sent me back to graduate school to finish my Ph.D. (1971), after which I worked for three years at an Air Force base near Madrid, Spain.

My marriage fell apart, due in part to my relational naivete at the time, and I left the service, taking a job as a psychologist for San Bernardino County in California in 1975, because I thought Southern California would be a good place to pursue further psychotherapy training and get my own therapy. Quickly assigned to lead the doctoral clinical psychology internship program in the Department of Mental Health, I helped the program achieve national accreditation. I was given several county awards as outstanding psychologist of the year in the Department. I also analyzed pending state legislation for its impact on the department and headed up a small Quality Assurance audit team. I helped as an oral examiner of psychology license applicants for the State of California for several years, and served as President of the Inland Psychological Association (for whom I also served as Ethics Chair). I revised the By-Laws of both the Inland Psychological Association and the Education and Training Division of the California Psychological Association. I became board-certified (American Board of Professional Psychology) in clinical psychology, participated as a board-certification examiner for others, and served as President of the American Academy of Clinical Psychology for several years. For part of my time in San Bernardino, I also had a small private practice.

My second marriage resulted in twenty-seven good years together, some of those helping to shepherd two fine children into productive adulthood, before my wife died of lung cancer in 2013. I have two fine (step) grandchildren from that marriage. My current partner, whom I have known for 56 years now, starting in the Air Force, is Diana Peterson—definitely my soul mate and the love of my life.

My passion as a psychologist was psychotherapy, and I trained over 200 interns and 100 post-doctoral psychologists in knowing themselves well and using that knowledge to help clients. After retirement in 2006, I turned to further philosophy studies in a search to put together all I had learned about people into some principles for how to have the best life possible ("how to live"), which is detailed in my 2023 book *Live Wisely, Deeply, and Compassionately*. I believe that wisdom can be pursued and can help us to understand ourselves and others and make the best decisions we can, while living deeply (fully experiencing life and one's emotions) prepares us to deal adaptively with life's ups and downs. Compassion (deeply understanding the lives of others and wishing less suffering for them) is what we need most in this country in order to work together as citizens amicably. For the past several years I have been active in the Religious Society of Friends (the Quakers), who practice radical equality (that all are equal) and seek solutions to problems that are acceptable to all (instead of simply letting majority vote rule).

I have worked seriously and hard over the years to become the kind of person I wanted to be, and I'm pleased with the result! I believe (judging myself in comparison to others) that I am (and would be seen by others as) thoughtful, intelligent, quiet, calm, reasonable, fair, friendly, articulate, trustworthy, honest, responsible, consistent, accepting, cooperative, self-confident, self-aware, compassionate, and empathic. I have good self-control and manage my emotions well. I look for the best in people. I am "nice" but can be very tough in standing up for what I believe in. I have a relatively objective view of reality and can make good decisions. I insist on having adequate data (whenever possible) before coming to conclusions (which is probably frustrating to some). I have good self-esteem and like myself. I have good, happy relations with others in general, and I appreciate real closeness and intimacy. I enjoy making others happy, and I believe firmly in the "win-win" principle of relationships. I am practiced at finding common understandings between parties and finding solutions based on these realistic understandings. I believe that all of these qualities and abilities will serve me well in the position of President of these United States!

FUNDAMENTAL PRINCIPLES OF GOOD GOVERNMENT

This platform addresses structural and process issues that relate to the health and functionality of government—in this particular case, our democratic government, which includes concerns about our electoral process, our legislative process, and some current situational issues facing the United States. I believe that honest, fair, and decent behavior on the part of candidates and office holders will both win votes and lead to the election of the best qualified candidate. The key principles embodied in this platform are *honesty, fairness, integrity, desire to serve the citizens (rather than simply wanting to get elected), desire to serve all citizens (rather than just the ones who agree with me), voter education and empowerment, and full and open communication about a candidate's motives and intentions.*

Here are the values and principles of human relations and government practice that guide my offer to become President and will guide every one of my actions as President.

BASIC HUMAN PSYCHOLOGICAL NEEDS

As a psychologist, I am convinced that in order to feel comfortable in society and happy as a person, we all need to feel relatively safe and to feel valued by others. The way we treat each other on a daily basis and all actions of government should aim to further these ends—that everyone can feel safe and valued. I believe that people are basically good and that most are decent people who are willing to work together as equals to make better lives for all.

Citizens become disheartened and angry when they feel insecure about basic living needs (when they cannot earn enough to have a decent life and therefore feel like they are not an equal part of society) and when they feel demeaned by other citizens for who they are or what they have.

Our current wealth inequality (made possible only through our very productive capitalism) tells people at the lower end of the income spectrum that they are not worth as much as those with more, and this is destructive to their self-esteem and makes them less willing to cooperate as a part of society.

EQUALITY

Society works best when there is basic equality among all citizens, by which I mean that citizens are valued equally as citizens in various ways–

- our laws apply to everyone equally,
- everyone has sufficient opportunities in life to feel that they can have a good life,
- no one is favored above anyone else by government,
- everyone is expected to contribute significantly to our well-being and defense,
- everyone has opportunity to voice his/her needs and to have impact on how the country makes its decisions,
- everyone is treated by everyone else as a basic equal, with respect and courtesy.

RESPECT

Every citizen should treat every other citizen with respect and courtesy at all times. One of the problems that led to the recent populist movement (including the Jan. 6 riot) is that the political elites (professors, pastors, CEO's, government officials, think-tank contributors news analysts, "experts") have tended more and more over the last two decades to look down on working class people and to trumpet a meritocratic attitude that holds people themselves as responsible when they are not doing as well as they would like to in life (ignoring all developmental, environmental, and historical factors that have impacted them).

STATUS

The aspects of a society's status hierarchy that induce everyone to tolerate their lot in life (including that some get more than others) are useful in reducing the amount of anger over the unequal outcomes in life and the seeming unfairness of it all that is expressed in crime, victimhood, and refusing to try. However, the aspects of that status hierarchy that allow those higher up to feel "better than" than those below them are destructive to a democratic society. Unfortunately many people want to feel "better than" others, basically to make up for not feeling valued enough themselves. I will work toward inculcating an attitude that says that everyone is basically equal as persons and has value just for being alive and part of our society.

These values point directly to my way of dealing with relationships, which will be exactly the same way if I am President as they are now.

- approach people positively and treat them well and fairly, expecting good treatment in return
- expect the best from people (the best they are capable of) and treat them as if they can produce that
- assist them in any way I can to live the best way possible (in relationships, in work, etc.)
- include them in my decisions that affect them and work out jointly acceptable solutions that benefit everyone

I believe that people are basically good and that in almost all cases, "bad" behavior is the result of unfortunate conditioning and exposure during one's early years. People always and naturally do what they consider to be in their best interest, so helping people to act in positive and healthy ways is a matter of showing them that more positive behaviors (treating other people well and fairly, being open to positive relating with others) is in their best interest. (The ability to delay gratification reasonably and the belief that taking turns will benefit everyone equally in the long run are needed in order for an individual to share (to let other people have their way or get what they want some of the time, so that we can get our way at other times), and some people will need to change their attitudes and beliefs in this regard in order to participate effectively in a cooperative society.)

In human morality, we seek to develop and codify ideas about not harming others. (Not harming others and therefore not being harmed ourselves is the justification for having morality at all.) Our justice system is based on redressing harm that has taken place. Other customs, such as dietary or social customs, are arbitrary and are not necessary parts of morality or religion (when seen as dealing with the individual's relationship with the divine).

I am calling myself "a compassionate president" (if elected, of course) as something that distinguishes me from other candidates. Compassion is being aware of the suffering of others and wishing for that suffering to be lessened. I am very aware of the suffering of our middle class and working class citizens, due to globalization and our increasing wealth inequity, and I am determined to do something about it, through people understanding each other better and learning the value of compromises. I care about how Americans feel about themselves and about their fellow citizens. I am also aware of the suffering caused by our culture wars and political power struggles, and I wish very much to reduce that suffering and conflict. Acting on my sense of compassion, I will treat everyone as equals, with respect and courtesy, irrespective of status in our society. This also means that I will not rant and rave about anyone or any group or insult them, even when I speak out about behavior that is adding to our collective suffering.

Wanting to reduce unnecessary suffering through improving how we relate to each other and how we take care of each other is my only motive for seeking the presidency. I'm not interested in power or glory (though I must admit I do like recognition). I assume that many of our elected representative are aware, also, or somewhat aware of this suffering, but they seem to treat it as something that no one can change or that can be changed only by one side or the other "wining," and I disagree wholeheartedly with this. I know that something can be done, if our citizens and representatives are willing.

Other Opinions

Equality and letting people think for themselves are both dangerous (equality because without being controlled, people will not be responsible, and independent thinking because it leads to chaos). An emphasis on love and positivity would simply give people the message that they can act any way they want. People who know better should seek positions of power so they can control things. The people don't know what is best for the country, so their input makes them feel better but should have no impact on government decisions (except for getting us re-elected). The power and status of those in control is necessary to keep our society stable. Without strong authority and a strong leader, the country is lost. Strong leaders contribute stability and a positive reputation to the constituency and should be allowed to stay in office as long as the voters want them.

HOW DEMOCRATIC GOVERNMENT CAN FUNCTION BEST

A democracy (or a republic) will be most democratic if it seeks to actualize a number of key principles.

(1) The desires of each citizen for the country should carry as much weight as the desires of any other citizen. Citizens with greater status, power,

or wealth should have no greater ability to influence the government than the man (or woman) in the street. Our government has been improperly more greatly influenced by the desires of the "elites" – wealthier people, academics, and groups that promise to deliver votes (political parties, PACS, etc.), and this has alienated significant segments of the population and even promoted the formation of a few local militias that are not loyal to the government.

(2) The best decisions by government should be made after gathering the desires and views of as many citizens as possible. This may be done through internet straw polls, conventional polling, or by inviting free-form feedback from citizens on a special website. The phrasing of questions in these polls must not bias the outcomes. A particular problem for our government currently is that is improperly influenced by those who speak the loudest and those who have a single emotionally-related issue that they advocate for. These people are, however, only a small portion of the citizenry (perhaps ten percent?), and the views and desires of the other ninety percent are not investigated or considered (since they are not motivated to speak up voluntarily). The small number of citizens voting (particularly in primary elections) supports the influence of the ten percent, which is why active assessment of the entire citizenry's views is imperative.

(3) The representatives of the people in Congress should vote individually for legislation according to their own estimates of what is best for the country and their own constituency and should not band together in power blocs for voting (like the Democratic Party or the Republican Party), since voting according to the views of others deprives the country of creativity and deprives a representative's constituents of proper representation. There is no advantage for democracy for Congress to be divided into two political blocs that spend much of their time fighting each other for power.

Congress would be serving the country better if we did not have this major split, which most people probably believe is part of the Constitution but which is actually the creation of Congress itself as members sought ways to create larger and larger power blocs in order to get their own way. I believe that there are a number of Congresspersons who do work reasonably well "across the aisle," and those who are not so inclined are in my opinion not fit to be in Congress. Structural changes could help, such as seating Congresspersons randomly instead of dividing the chamber into two sides! The power of speakers of the House and Senate should be greatly curtailed, as there is no benefit to the country to having leaders of such huge power blocs. It would be better to have co-leaders (one from each party, with different views) at the very least. Similarly, committee chairs should be assigned for knowledge and merit rather than having the party "in power" filling the majority of those chairs. And, for any party conventions and elections within parties (like primaries), the parties should pay for everything (you as taxpayers should not pay at all for party functions, as you do now for primary elections).

(4) Just as the President is restricted to two terms in office, Congresspersons and Supreme Court judges should be term-limited as well (Representatives—four terms; Senators—two terms; Judges—twenty years). Continuity in office has its merits, but it also limits the creativity coming from that office. The longer a person is in an office, the more power he/she accumulates, and power can become the reason for staying in the office, rather than service to all the people. The personality of an incumbent can become symbolic of the whole constituency (e.g., Huey Long in Louisiana), which also limits new ideas and therefore the overall progress of the constituency.

THE PRESIDENCY—THE REALITY (OR UNREALITY) OF PRESIDENTIAL POWER

Our government did not start out having the presidency be as important as it has become. In this country we have moved gradually to view the President like a king. Many citizens tend to think the President should be able to do anything and change just about anything for citizens' benefit, but that is not reality. Congress determines the law, and the President carries it out. Candidates for the presidency (and for other offices as well) speak as if they can do all sorts of things that only Congress can do (and citizens are led to believe that the Supreme Court's job is do decide what is right, when its only job is actually to decide whether laws (often the Constitution) have been violated and not whether those laws were "right" or "wrong.")

Voters should understand that the President has limited power, given our tripartite governmental structure (legislative, executive, and judicial branches, with checks and balances to see that no one branch dominates). Presidents can, though, to some extent set the tone for society and identify useful foci to help us to become a better society. As President I will champion the values and actions that I think will be best for the country, but the President does not make the law, and I will be clear to the people about what I cannot do. I will not make impossible promises but will indicate how I would proceed to work on good solutions to our problems and issues.

HONESTY

In order to work together effectively and amicably, we must be able to trust each other, and the key to trust is honesty. You are no doubt aware of politicians who will say whatever they think people would like to hear at the moment, even if they themselves don't even believe it, with little commitment to carrying out what they have promised if elected. I will always reveal my motives for every proposal, and I will always say what I mean (clearly and unambiguously) and mean what I say. If my views change on a topic, I will let you know and tell you why.

Part of the "prevailing wisdom" regarding elections is that one must minimize offending anyone, because that would arouse single-issue voters to vote against one. This results in candidates always speaking vaguely and avoiding specifics, so that you don't really know whether to vote for them or not. I will always tell you what I think. Candidates don't reveal themselves to you because they want you to vote for them regardless of their views and qualifications (i.e., regardless of how you would be impacted if they were elected). This is a recipe for electing the wrong people! In return for getting the full information about me, I ask you to look at the total of my positions when you judge my candidacy. Don't just reject me because you disagree with one or two of my positions. You will probably never know what the other candidates' positions are on those issues anyway!

From my observations, there are many candidates who apparently believe that people are honest only when it is to their advantage and that lying is OK if it helps you get what you want. I believe that we should be honest with each other because it makes for a better life for us all, and because we care about each other. "Let the buyer beware" is a cheap way of sellers evading responsibility for being dishonest. I believe that a seller should have the honesty and the caring about the buyer to tell the buyer both the pros and the cons of the product.

Also, exaggeration is used frequently by politicians, apparently to make things seem simple and to vilify the other side. Doing this is dishonest. Statements on policy issues should explain the reasons for one's position *and* the reasons for other positions as well.

Other Opinions

Only tell voters what they absolutely need to know, because there is no way to integrate 330,000,000 different views on things. If you let people see who you are, they will use it to destroy you, so leaders need to pretend to be who the voters want, and it's ethical to say whatever pleases voters regardless of whether it is true. No one really believes what candidates say, so it's OK to exaggerate to make voters feel better in the moment.

RESPONSIBLITY

We must be able to count on all government employees and functionaries, and they must all be accountable—even Presidents and Congresspersons. No one is above the law.

It is also important that decision-makers in government have some skin in the game (or at least the feeling of having skin in the game), so that they consider how every decision is going to affect all citizens and so that decisions and rule-making are not divorced from real life. It would be useful if every decision by Congress, for example, was made with knowledge by Senators and Representatives of how much it would add to or reduce the taxes of all citizens. (This prediction would be made public, too, of course.) It would also be useful (though we will never do this) if all Congresspersons who voted for a particular bill based on their belief about the effects of the bill would commit to reimburse the government some amount of money if their predictions turn out to be false (like betting on your own decision-making).

Other Opinions
Our systems are too complex for anyone to figure out who is really responsible for anything, so it is OK for leaders to blame someone else and to support irresponsible positions so that they can get re-elected. An unbalanced federal budget is not a problem, because people in future generations will be paying for it, not us. People want things for themselves now and will not vote for politicians who expect voters to act like adults.

FAIRNESS

Every citizen deserves equal treatment under the law and under the regulations of every part of the government. No one will get favored status with me in getting what they want—not for having money, not for contributing to campaigns, not for being related to me, and not for simply complaining or rioting. Any favoritism on the part of government employees will be grounds for discipline. No one should get special favors or deals from the government, because that means that some other citizens will get less from their government or will have to make up in taxes the costs of those special deals that others get. There are many candidates whose preference is to make special deals in order to make political allies and get votes, and to keep their special deals secret.

It is absolutely essential to clear up "the swamp" in Washington (the mass of secret deals and influence-peddling). Mr. Trump did almost nothing about this, after promising that he would. This can only be done by eliminating all special deals and special access to government by anyone. Lobbyists will have no influence in my administration, except for any good ideas that they might bring that will be to the advantage of all citizens. People who contribute to my candidacy should not do so to get increased access to the government (which they will not get) but should do so because they want everyone to be treated equally and fairly. Our government should not be government of money and deals.

Other Opinions

Nothing is really fair in life, and society is really just a big arena for conflict in which the stronger will dominate and take advantage of the weaker. We have to pretend that things are fair to prevent a revolution, but sadly that is just a pretense.

INTEGRITY

Every decision I make will be made with consideration for the desires and needs of all segments of the citizenry. Government works best when everyone benefits equally, and every citizen counts. Sometimes an act of government is aimed specifically at a problem of only one group, but I will not act for the benefit of one group unless it is with the assumption and intent that every other group will in its turn benefit in the future.

I will enforce all laws passed by Congress and signed into law and will not drop enforcement of any due to public pressure. I will pressure Congress to change laws, even popular ones, rather than pass on what should be its responsibility to the Executive branch or to the Supreme Court out of fear of voter reaction.

Our system of Democrats and Republicans each pulling the country in a different direction brings their different conceptions of our future into relief, but trying to dominate is anti-democratic because it assumes that one group in our society should be able to impose its will on everyone else. In a healthy democracy, no group can dominate, and every decision should involve attempts to benefit all citizens, not just some. Getting a majority of the vote is not sufficient justification for enacting legislation, since the impact on all groups and parts of the country must be the key justification.

Other Opinions

Politicians have to do what is expedient, so you have to wiggle out of seeming responsible in the eyes of voters. They won't remember what you said before the election, they won't find out how you vote in Congress, and they won't remember much of what you actually do when in office.

SERVING THE CITIZENS IS MORE IMPORTANT THAN GETTING ELECTED

Many politicians justify misleading voters by saying that you can't do anything for the country unless you get elected—meaning that they don't reveal anything that might offend some group of voters. I believe that a candidate while campaigning should show the citizens exactly who he or she will be if elected. Since the foundations of my campaign are honesty and integrity, I will illustrate these in my campaign behavior. In providing information to voters about myself, I will describe exactly how I will conduct the business of the Presidency. I will indicate my current understanding of various issues, as well as the policy implications of that understanding. Most candidates focus on making promises and on symbolic outcomes (build a wall, leave the Paris climate agreement) that may or may not prove to be the best thing to do when the candidate is actually in a position to do anything.

I believe that my ideas and values will lead to betterment of life for the people of this country, but I also recognize that others may have different beliefs in this regard. I will consider all of these opinions and beliefs in deciding what will indeed be best for all citizens and for the country. These considerations will be scrupulously conducted in a respectful and thoughtful manner, even when feelings about the issues are strong. I will pursue the course of action that will most greatly benefit the most people and the nation as a whole in every case, after all of the long-term as well as the short-term consequences of the decision are evaluated. What is best for the country will be the highest priority, not what will get me re-elected or get me more campaign contributions.

The view that elected officials should work to obtain as much government money for their constituents as possible will be discouraged, since that places them in direct competition with all other constituencies in the nation for the money. I will work toward fair and even distribution of resources among all groups and parts of the country. This process of distribution must be viewed long term, though, since in some years some parts of the citizenry will benefit more and in other years other parts of the citizenry will benefit more, but all must work for equitable distribution over the long haul rather than competing every year to get all they can. All recipients of monies and the amounts and purposes of such monies will be published for all citizens annually (and I will tell you where to find it).

I want voters to try to figure out which candidate will serve the country best, but we do not have good mechanisms for making this happen. Sound bites and slogans (Make America Great Again; Hope Is On the Way) are designed to be attractive but tell you little about the candidate (Is he thoughtful? Is she honest? Will he be fair? Is she willing to compromise, or will she be part of the gridlock in Washington?). Unfortunately our system currently gives the greatest advantage to the candidate that raises the most money, and this may well not be the best candidate. Furthermore, Congresspersons, I'm told, when in office spend up to a third of their time *every day* trying to raise money for the next campaign. This is a terrible waste of their time, which is supposed to be used for legislative decision-making. I accept the necessity of advertising but only for purposes of actually informing the public, not to try to sweet talk people into thinking that I am what I am not. I will emphasize getting voters useful information rather than having the most ads on TV, and I believe that the country will be better served if we reduce the amount of money going into campaigns in general. I will support making campaigns for national offices only six months long, to encourage all candidates to focus on communicating what they want to say to voters rather than posturing and fighting among themselves. This is not an infringement of free speech but a step toward focusing voters on electing the best candidate for the job rather than on popularity and voter manipulation.

We are seeing the lackluster results of a system that assumes that personal desires for fame or adulation are the principal motives for candidates for major offices. The most powerful factor in determining the behavior of incumbents currently is positioning to be re-elected, which takes away the power to do something for the country that is not yet popular but is essential for the future of our society. I am not asserting that the voters don't know best, but elected officials in a representative democracy must always take what the voters say and want and find ways that will actually give the voters what is in their best interest even if that seems different at the time.

The bottom line is that we would probably be better off electing people who do not particularly want the offices in question but who are urged by others to run because they would do a good job. Candidates who personally want to be elected (for self-esteem, prestige, fame, adulation, etc.) will spend time and energy to get these personal benefits that would be better spent in solving problems for the country.

Other Opinions
Winning is everything. You have to get elected no matter how you do it, before you can have any influence. Being elected President is the greatest achievement for a citizen, so the desire to do it must be a good thing (follow your dreams!).

SERVING ALL CITIZENS AND NOT ONLY ONE'S SUPPORTERS

The government must serve all of the people of this country, at all times. Therefore, it is not in the best interest of the country for parties or administrations to use their power to promulgate the ideas and wishes of only their members or supporters. In the past, this has produced an inefficient zig-zag course of action from election to election, as each party tries to benefit only its members when in power (and force everyone else to live according to what it believes). This behavior also tends to turn politics into a competition in which only some of the citizens can "win" at any given time. All political groups must give up the idea that their purpose is to force everyone to live the life that their group prefers, instead recognizing that all mature adults have a legitimate concept of what makes a good life and that government should make a good life possible for as many citizens as it can. (All candidates should make clear to voters what kind of society the candidate will promote.)

Every time some individual or small group gets a favor from government, it works to the disadvantage of some other citizens, who will have to pay more taxes to pay for the favor or will be excluded from some benefit that the favored person or group gets (a zoning change, a tax exemption, etc.). This is not fair, and I will not do it or support it. In order to trust government, we must be able to believe that no one is getting favors that work to our own disadvantage. I will also make public any secret deals that I know of that Congresspersons make that favor only their own constituency to the disadvantage of others.

I pledge to make all decisions and take all actions with due consideration for the beliefs and positions of *all* citizens. This will mean that each decision may displease some, but providing the greatest good for the greatest number, while avoiding harm to as many as possible, will be the guiding principle. I urge you as a voter to figure out which candidates will actually serve all citizens rather than just themselves and their supporters. *You* can influence where this country goes.

Pres. Trump campaigned against the Washington "swamp," which I understand to be the complex interrelationships between elected and appointed officials and various persons (like lobbyists) who wish to influence the government in ways that will give special benefit to them or their clients or employers. Mr. Trump did little if anything to "drain the swamp," since he seemed to operate to favor those who support him. This is, of course, "natural" for human beings, but it is the opposite of draining the swamp. Mr. Trump favors making deals, but I favor up-or-down voting on all well-discussed proposals that aim to benefit everyone, not just the deal-makers.

Other Opinions

Only if you have power can you accomplish anything, and your power is multiplied if you stand with others, like your party, who think and act the same. You must get re-elected, and the best way to do this is to keep your "base" of voters enthusiastic. The best way to do that is to criticize and put down the other side.

GOVERNMENT BY PRINCIPLES RATHER THAN CABAL

Human beings naturally form friendship and alliance groups, but this practice harms democratic government if any official favors his friendship and alliance groups over the country or any one of its citizens (which would fly in the face of the principle of equality among citizens with respect to government). This could happen in considering applications, making decisions, the wording of public statements, etc. While I will no doubt have alliances and favorite advisors, I will strive to make every decision based on what is good for the country, and I will insist on this from every person in the Executive Branch. Some will be unhappy with this, since there are some who are in it for themselves and not for the country.

Other Opinions

No one can do this. You cannot get anything done without the cooperation of a bunch of people, all of whom expect favors back from you for their cooperation. The government runs on trading favors.

AN INFORMED CITIZENRY—VOTER EDUCATION

Legislators who serve themselves rather than their constituents avoid dealing with issues that could anger some voters, even if dealing intelligently and fairly with those issues would be in the best interest of everyone (e.g., the immigration issue). This is the primary reason for Congressional inaction when action is sorely needed. I will avoid this cowardly position and will openly and diligently work toward action even on unpopular or sensitive issues that could alienate certain voters (though only after I have heard their input). The guiding principle will be seeking the greatest good for all citizens, rather than attempting to impose on others any view or position of any one group of people.

In order that voters not vote for a "pig in a poke," I am publishing this compendium of positions and proposals on all currently relevant issues, regardless of their popularity or of their potential to alienate certain voters. There will be no secrets regarding what I will do if elected that will be purposely obscured or withheld from voters. Campaign speeches and publications will give a comprehensive view of my political philosophy, rather than focusing only on single issues that appeal to various small groups of voters. Position and proposal publications will be provided to those media who are willing to publish them *in their entirety* (print or on-line), and they will be published on-line and provided in print to all who request them (assuming sufficient campaign funds to do so!). Since television ads cannot give this comprehensive understanding of issues, I will provide it in other ways (such as my website—www.ebbeforpresident.com).

Since an educated and informed electorate is the best guarantee of good government, *I will provide weekly, even-handed updates to the people on the work of the government, rather than giving emotional appeals without facts, aimed at maintaining voter support for actions that voters might question if the facts were provided. I will give you the key arguments on both sides (or all sides) and not just what I think is best.* The designation of "classified information," which has been used by some administrations to keep secret from citizens information that might bring them criticism, will be used only for true national security reasons.

In the interest of voter education and progress in general, I will invite all sides to add to my updates their reasons for supporting their positions. We should be finding the best solutions—those that will benefit the most citizens–no matter who proposes them. I will also reveal the hypocrisy of anyone who says that he supports something that he does not really support. There will be no secret backroom deals by me. Congresspersons (particularly speakers of the House and Senate) who are blocking important legislation will be identified publicly. I will keep nothing secret from you, unless it is for the purpose of protecting citizens' confidentiality. Being in Congress should generally not be a career, as this leads to inappropriate levels of influence and to unwillingness to change.

I will seek to establish a news/politics media outlet that presents both liberal and conservative views, with a mixed staff and interaction between staff on both sides. We'll see how many people want all sides of an issue and how many don't want to hear more than one!

See "Ad Fontes" (on-line) for a company that evaluates bias in social media and news outlets.

Other Opinions
The issues that beset our country are too complicated for voters to understand, and the real solutions to them are unpalatable to voters, so the name of the game is look good, regardless of what you really believe or will do if elected.

FIGHTING VS. COMPROMISE

Our constant fighting in government is unproductive and divisive. Finding and being willing to live with effective compromises are key to making democracy work. (See the section below "ACCEPTING COMPROMISE AS THE NORM FOR OUR DEMOCRACY.")

COMPETITION

Competition is often lauded in our society as the key ingredient in advancement and progress, and in some specific instances it is helpful in that way. However, to encourage competition in everything is bad for our emotional health, since then we don't have enough sense of security in our relationships and connections. Competition among children is natural, as they try to figure out how they fit into social structures or try to get more of parents' love than their siblings, but as we mature, these motives for competition should fade. After that, competition, should become more about doing one's best (competing against oneself or against some important standard) rather than trying to be better than someone else. Winning as evidence that one is better than others is destructive and self-defeating in the sense that no matter how good one is, there is always someone else who is a little better. No one who has a world record holds it forever. Everyone ages. Competition that asserts that one is untouchable is foolish, as everyone is vulnerable in a number of ways.

For the sake of our fellow citizens and our own emotional health, competition should be "reasonable" rather than cut-throat. Employers who pit workers against each other are making their lives worse. The only one who benefits from that competition is the employer. We as individuals must have the good sense not to compete when it is actually destructive and to keep it "friendly" competition if it is to be in any way entertaining. We have so much competition in our society that I will focus things instead of cooperation and on appreciation of what we can do rather than on who is "better."

ALLIANCES AND VOTE TRADING

It is natural for people, including freshman Congresspersons, to form alliances to help each other. Unfortunately, this leads to vote trading, where a Congressperson agrees to vote for a proposal of the other person if that other person will vote for something the Congressperson wants. (Both of our two major parties are the ultimate examples of this.) This gives a distorted picture of the actual support for any proposal. I will speak against vote trading and encourage every elected official to vote their own positions and/or conscience. If a proposal doesn't matter to them, then to abstain is the proper course. I will encourage every elected official to vote for what he or she believes, regardless of what his/her party wants. Voting "along party lines" will be irrelevant and anathema to me.

Other Opinions
You can't get anything done in Congress without enough allies to pass what you want. All elected official are working only for their own ends, so you have to give them something in order to get something (their support).

WORKING TOGETHER

Our two-party system and our national inclination to fight rather than talk have combined to result in political stalemate and frittering away our energies on the fighting rather than accepting that in a country as diverse as ours, we must work toward solutions to problems that most citizens can live with—solutions in which everyone benefits to some degree and no one gets exactly what he/she wants. To gain back more of a sense of national kinship we need to focus on working together to find the best solutions possible at the current time for our problems. I will press Congress to adopt this attitude and will assist by meeting frequently with Congressional leaders to suggest effective compromises. The American people should know what progress is being made on these problems, and I will suggest that Congress give them a monthly update (even if only something like "House Appropriations Committee still developing proposal" or "Reconciliation in progress"), and I will provide this kind of information to citizens as much as possible.

We need to structure our political work to include more opportunities to work together rather than spending all of our time crafting strategies for defeating the other side. Toward this end, I will seek (1) having a vice-president who has a different political view than mine (Liz Cheney?, Adam Kinzinger?), or having the second-highest vote-getter be the vice-president (as it used to be), and (2) gathering in the White House full-time advisors that include all political views.

Other Opinions
Competition is good for everyone. Seeking to win is very important to Americans. Mixing up people of different beliefs to work together will only confuse people and lead to a mish-mash of policies. We like our national fighting, so let's keep doing it.

NATIONAL SERVICE

Since our military has become all volunteer, without a draft, we have lost a major process through which citizens learned how we all are part of one nation and one effort to have the best lives that we can. To counteract this and bring working together back into focus, I will call for a one-year mandatory period of national service for all young citizens. This could be accomplished by one year of work in the Peace Corps or the Teacher Corps, as a volunteer aide to a Congressperson or other federal official in

Washington, working with other development agencies in the U.S., or by a two-year term in the military (two years because that is probably the minimum that the military needs in order to train people and also get some service contribution from them).

Other Opinions

A year of service would interrupt our youth in their eager progress toward their working careers—no one will support that. Only wussies would seek to help others at the sacrifice of their own interests.

IS DEMOCRACY REALLY WHAT WE WANT?

This platform is constructed to aid democracy and democratic principles (above), but is democracy what the citizens in general want? There is concern currently about challenges to democracy from President Trump in particular, since he prefers to ignore the law when he can get away with it and would like to be an all-powerful ruler, unrestricted by the Constitution.

Each citizen must make a fundamental choice between rule by one (autocracy, dictatorship, or monarchy) and rule by all (democracy or representative government). Rule by a king or dictator is simpler, but the reason that people have slowly moved away from monarchy is that a single ruler inevitably favors his/her own friends and allies over other citizens and can inflict any pain, even death, on any citizen he/she chooses whenever he/she wants. The unpredictability of this and the constant danger of the king turning on you makes most people wish to have any ruler constrained by rules that are determined by the people.

Democracy is more difficult to maintain, since it involves having every citizen speak about what he/she wants and then trying to combine these wishes to benefit as many citizens as possible while harming the fewest possible. Democracies move slowly and can get lost in legal wrangles, but democracy is still more desirable to most people than other forms of government.

When things are difficult in a democracy, many are tempted to elect a strong leader who can supposedly control the chaos. Pres. Trump presented himself as this strong leader and cleverly supported the feelings of alienation of a considerable segment of the population whose economic situation had declined over the last twenty years of globalization and who resented more liberal people for trying to change the country's morals without their having a say in it. If we as a country do not do something about the economic situation of this pro-dictator segment, its members will continue to question whether democracy is best for the U.S. (As you can see from this platform, I believe that democracy is only going to work well for us if it is a more compassionate democracy—a democracy with more heart. Our society is too complicated now to expect each individual to cope with it all (healthcare, insurances, a stable career, taxes), and unless we care more about each other, our democracy and our capitalist system will continue to ignore people's needs and become more and more heartless and more and more vulnerable to a dictator's promises.)

Once again, you as a citizen must choose between the difficulties (and benefits) of democracy and the dangers (and benefits) of having a dictator. What's it to be?

In the following sections, I will describe in some detail the issues I will focus most on if I am elected. It may sound idealistic (and it is), but bear in mind that even if these things cannot be accomplished during my term as President, I will push to bring them into the public consciousness as serious issues for the country that need to be addressed when we find the will power to do so! Here are the issues.

- restoring equality among citizens (in the chapter above on principles of good government)
- restoring amity and acceptance among citizens
- bringing truth to politics
- diminishing the power of the two major political parties
- establishing compromise as the norm for our democracy
- reforming our tax system and attitudes
- making elections about who can do the job best
- jobs for all and a wage for a decent life
- encouraging civil discourse on political issues among citizens
- revising our immigration policy
- encouraging better emotional health for citizens

AMITY AND ACCEPTANCE AMONG CITIZENS

"Amity is defined as "friendship; peaceful harmony." We could certainly use more amity right now! I would like to encourage in all of us a feeling of caring about the feelings and welfare of other citizens. Feeling that others care is a very valuable component of feeling valued and comfortable in life, and these are feelings that we need more of in our society. Wouldn't it be great if we could trust others to care about us and about how they treat us? You would expect salesmen to be honest with you, bankers not to risk your money unnecessarily, leaders to stand up for you when needed even if they lost popularity by doing that, and coaches not to favor their own kids over yours. We could have this if we all cared about and took seriously the feelings and needs of others.

In general, all of the world's great religions teach dealing with others in a positive and caring way. This is clear in Christianity and Buddhism and is true also of more liberal forms of Islam.

I want to encourage you and all other citizens to be positive toward and have a caring attitude with respect to every other human being, including family, coworkers, organizational colleagues, fellow citizens, and even those you dislike. Taking this attitude with you through the day will brighten your day and that of everyone you interact with. Approaching everyone with a positive attitude, expecting good things to happen, hoping for a mutually useful and emotionally positive interaction, in part will create the very thing you are wanting. Treating others positively and offering an interaction that is maximally useful and emotionally gratifying tends to induce others to do the same, and when both people have this attitude, good things can happen. Those who feel better because of your attitude toward them will tend to carry this forward into their other interactions. This is the opposite of approaching others suspiciously, self-protectively, and predicting the worst or expecting to be degraded or tricked—attitudes that are created by experiences of being lied to, put down, and degraded.

CARING FOR OTHERS

An attitude of caring for others benefits everyone. We like feeling cared about, we feel good about caring for others, and in caring relationships, all naturally cooperate for the good of everyone. In our complex and interdependent society, there are no citizens who do not impinge on your welfare in some way. Think of all the people it takes to make the products you like to buy and supply you with electricity and water. They are essential for your way of life, and it is appropriate to be glad that they are there doing their jobs. Feeling glad about how you benefit motivates you to care about their welfare as well.

A caring attitude has these essentials—

- caring about the feelings and welfare of others (as evidenced by feeling pain when others are hurt)
- feeling positively toward others (including initially assuming the best rather than the worst about others)
- feeling warmly toward others
- seeing ourselves as basic equals with others rather than superior to them
    wanting good things for others
    wanting things to go well for others
    wanting others to be happy (and not to suffer)
    treating others well
- giving others basic acceptance

If you care about another person, you want the best for him or her—i.e. for him/her to benefit from your interaction, as well as yourself (the desirable "win-win" situation). If you view another person with care, you will be honest with him, because that is necessary for him to get maximum benefit from your interaction. This includes warning the person about things that you know that could result in harm to him, even if by informing him you may lower your potential outcomes in the interaction (e.g., a car salesman pointing out a weakness of the car he wants to sell). If you view another person with caring, you will be responsible with her—i.e., do what you say you'll do and conform to your society's general expectations for what is appropriate. If you care about others, you will give them the freedom you yourself want—to be allowed to be himself/herself as long as that it not harming others. If you care about others, you will act toward them with integrity—e.g., being truly yourself with the other person rather than pretending to be other than you really are.

If you have a caring attitude, you will not try to take advantage of others, since in caring for others, we want good things for them. If you have a caring attitude, you will not try to force others to do what you want (e.g., through threats, shaming, or extortion), because that would not be good for them.

If we care about the feelings and welfare of others, we do not want them to suffer. "Caring" here means that what others are experiencing matters to us, even if it's only a little. Caring implies that how they feel "means something" to us. An example of "caring about" would be feeling some pain yourself when you see that person hurt.

If you feel good about yourself and believe in the positive results of your positive and caring attitude toward others, you can feel good about yourself and what you are doing regardless of any fearful or negative reactions of others to your efforts. Of course, we would like to benefit from interactions ourselves, but if you know that you are doing good by viewing others with care, then particular reactions to you need not be important.

We do not expect that anyone will "love" every other human being in an intimate and life-encompassing way, but we can have a caring attitude toward everyone we encounter or think about. Behavioral examples of the results of this attitude include—

- saying hello in the morning to coworkers you don't know instead of only to ones you know
- offering the loan of your jumper cables to a coworker you don't know well who is having trouble starting his car, without his asking you
- inquiring of your partner whether she is bored with the TV show you picked out
- encouraging children who are not your own in a sports game instead of encouraging only your own children
- feeling happy for a coworker who is promoted to a position you wanted (at the same time that you also feel disappointed for not getting it yourself)
- feeling sad for the many people in failed or dysfunctional countries who are facing hardship, and being willing to admit

as many to your country as possible to have a better life (though not so many that current citizens in your country will be harmed)

In order to care about others requires that you have enough caring in your own life (so as not to be jealous of the caring you try to give others), enough interpersonal skills to communicate and not offend, and the self-knowledge and self-control sufficient to manage your emotions so as not to harm others.

"Good" or "positive" interactions are defined as interactions in which both parties feel comfortable and safe (as a result of understanding each other and feeling treated appropriately by the other person) and in which, as a result, both parties are motivated to cooperate, as needed, to achieve mutually agreeable goals (in the physical world or simply goals of emotional benefit). We feel comfortable and safe if we feel understood and basically accepted and if the relating seems pleasant and encouraging. These interactions succeed through understanding and cooperation and result in minimum amounts of conflict and violence between people. These "good" interactions are enhanced by your caring for others.

Feeling Positively Toward Others

Caring for others includes wanting the other person to be happy and not to be suffering. This positive attitude toward others is marked by (1) a hope of positive relating with any and all others, (2) openness to positive relations with others, (3) approaching others in a manner that encourages positive relating (including assuming the best about others until proven otherwise), (4) interest in others' lives and methods of coping, (5) treating others in ways that promote positive relating (honesty, responsibility for one's emotions and behavior, acceptance, fairness, equality, compassion, self-control, autonomy), and (6) willingness to engage in cooperative, mutually beneficial projects and to be helpful to others, as possible. "Positive relations" refers to the affective quality of the relating—i.e., that the relating is pleasant, comfortable, accepting, and encouraging.

A negative attitude toward others consists of distrust, dislike, and distancing, even if subtle, and it is likely to result in a focus on taking advantage of others in order to get what one wants.

Positive relations with others are based most fundamentally in a desire for those relations to be positive. We can appreciate the many benefits of having positive relations with others, including greater trust, greater comfort, and better cooperation, but those who have been mistreated and deceived will naturally also feel some fear and resentment.

Our positive attitude toward others should be infused with understanding, based on our life experiences that have led us to empathically appreciate the difficulties that everyone has in coping with life, the inner struggles that we are all engaged in, and the imperfections of us all.

Relations will not be sincerely and openly positive unless both parties are open to positive relations. This means being genuinely open to relating, without fears (at least facing those fears) and other barriers blocking the way. We show each other this openness in our speech and facial expressions.

Our positive attitude must be conveyed to others. Think of people who make you feel positive and comfortable when they approach you, and imitate what they do. Smile and courteously recognize the presence of others. (This is the underlying function of the usually otherwise meaningless greetings "How's it going?" and "How are you?") Use a look or a few words to put others at their ease around you. Express interest in the other person. Show that you are comfortable with your imperfectness. Don't wait for others to do these things; do them yourself proactively. Most people will respond positively and appreciatively to these signals of openness to positive relating, and you will feel effective and good about yourself for your efforts. Approaching others with a neutral or negative attitude (neutrally waiting for them to show or prove themselves, or expecting negative relating and therefore giving nothing away or subtly warning others not to relate) kills most chances for positive relating and also "proves" to you what you feared – that it is too dangerous to relate.

The chances of having positive relations are increased significantly if we are interested in others' lives and ways of coping, so that all of our encounters automatically have something of interest to us, even if we don't yet have common interests, joint projects, or other similarities. Some people are naturally "psychologically minded" in this way, but the rest of us can at least to some extent develop this curiosity about others if we are willing. Since human beings around the world all cope with the same feelings, the same bodily abilities, limitations, and infirmities, and basically the same environmental challenges, we can always potentially learn useful things from how others on how to deal with life and its problems, if we are willing to look at what they know and how they cope, psychologically, physically, and culturally. We can learn much from others, as long as we can overcome our inherent tendency to overvalue what we are familiar with and to view everything else as inferior.

In order both to create and to nurture positive relating, it is necessary to treat others in ways that promote positive relating. Being honest with others and being responsible in your relating to them makes it possible for others to trust you and be comfortable being with you. Treating others well also includes being responsible for managing your emotions, rather than expecting others to change so that you won't have to feel any unpleasant feelings. Demonstrating empathy shows them that there is at least a chance that you can understand their experience and situation, and demonstrating appropriate self-control shows them that you may be able to manage your behavior so as not to hurt them. Accepting others as they are allows them to relax with you and to feel welcome and valued. Treating others fairly tells them that you will apply the same rules to yourself that you apply to them, so that they don't have to worry so much that you will take advantage of them. Treating them basically as equals tells them that you understand that they have the same basic value in the world and the same rights as you do, which once again underscores that you recognize their basic value. Treating others with compassion tells them that you understand their struggles and that you place a high value on their welfare. Taking care of yourself happily and effectively shows them that you are not likely to seek to be dependent on them.

Positive relations are nurtured by your willingness to engage in cooperative, mutually beneficial projects and to be helpful to others, as possible. Whether it is simply helping to raise a stuck window, organizing a benefit dinner-dance, or fighting side by side in a war, working together for mutually desired goals is naturally (evolutionarily) rewarding to human beings and can transform positive relating into friendship. Your empathy and compassion make helping a natural and enjoyable thing to do, and they even "justify" some personal sacrifices for the sake of others' welfare. Of course, sharing your wisdom with others and receiving theirs, in ways that can benefit both, is another possible cooperative, mutually beneficial project.

Feeling Warmly Toward Others

Feeling warmly toward others is a natural offshoot of caring for others. If we want the best for a person, we are almost certain to feel warmly toward him or her. This warmth is love radiating from us. It flows from love and is not something that can be produced or sought independent of love.

Seeing Ourselves As Basic Equals With Others

The desires of each citizen for the country should carry as much weight as the desires of any other citizen. Citizens with greater status, power, or wealth should have no greater ability to influence the government than the man (or woman) in the street. Our government has been improperly more greatly influenced by the desires of the "elites" – wealthier people, academics, and groups that promise to deliver votes (political parties, PACS, etc.), and this has alienated significant segments of the population and even promoted the formation of a few local militias that are not loyal to the government.

In order to feel the full measure of the concern and positive feelings that we can have toward others, it is necessary to see ourselves as basic equals with others – not to feel superior or inferior to them. If we see ourselves as superior to them, we will think that we deserve love and approval more than they do, which will limit the positive feelings that we could have toward them. If we see ourselves as inferior to them, we will almost certainly have some resentment over this, which will restrict the free flow of caring feelings that we could have for them.

Basic equality, however, does not mean enforced equality in every way. In the U.S., we say that everyone should have equality of opportunity and be treated equally under the law, while at the same time accepting that people's status and possessions will in no way be equal.

Treating others as equals communicates our respect for them, and the good will and trust that flow from this minimize conflicts and allow others to feel comfortable with us. If we view ourselves as equals with others, then it follows easily that we will treat others fairly.

Because of our insecurity and our dependence as young children, we seek to be special to caregivers—certainly more special than the other children in the family! Being special reassures us about being treated as well as possible and that we would not be the first children to suffer if resources were scarce. It is difficult to give up this specialness and the striving to be special, but if we are honest, we know that we don't deserve special treatment more than any other child does. Accepting this both leaves us a bit less secure but gives us opportunity to join with and empathize with those other children.

The same dynamic applies to status hierarchies, since these status hierarchies tell us where we stand in importance or value in relation to others. If we accept our placement in the hierarchy (which is to some degree inevitably arbitrary and is based on immature and materialistic values), then society can be stable. If we protest or try to move up in the hierarchy, it disturbs society and leads to conflict, but perhaps the hierarchy itself is the problem. Perhaps none of us is any more important or valuable than anyone else. If we really view ourselves as an equal in this sense, then we lose the possibility of feeling that we are better than others (which we use to "prove" that we are worth something), but we also lose the competition and resentments that go with the hierarchy, and we will be much more able to be loving and caring (as equals).

The imprint of our childhood experience as being the least valuable and least powerful in the family is very strong and difficult to rid ourselves of. As children we long to be as valued and powerful as adults, and many of us aspire to be more highly valued and more powerful than others, which leads to status competition and using force to get our way with others. If we accept the benefits of equality (greater social comfort, better alliances, greater acceptance from others), then we give up our opportunity to be better than others.

Our true value is in how we use the life we have and how we help others to live their lives better. Our competition should not be with others in trying to be more valuable than they are but with ourselves in our striving to be the best person that we can be. Instead of using winning, income, achievements, etc., as proof that we are valuable and more valuable than some others, equality leads us to start viewing everyone, including ourselves, in terms of what is really important (how we manage our lives and what we give to others). The essential and more valuable qualities or achievements of each of us are (1) taking good care of ourselves and those dependent on us and (2) doing things that contribute to the welfare of the total group. These are what we should want to be admiringly and gratefully remembered for. (The reason that we are so unsure of our value is that we know that the valuing that others have for us is not totally dependable. See my book *How To Feel Good About Yourself: Twelve Keys To Having Good Self-Esteem*.)

When we see ourselves as equal to others, we cease much of our comparing of ourselves with others in terms of status, attractiveness. money, etc., because what is really important is how we view ourselves and what we are doing to make our lives good, as well as the lives of those around us. Honestly focusing on ourselves and our lives leads to taking responsibility for what we can do for ourselves.

Wanting Good Things For Others

If we have caring feelings for others, then we want them to be happy, have a good life, and not to suffer. Our empathy alerts us to how others feel, and we feel a little worse ourselves when we see others unhappy or suffering. Based on our caring feelings, we naturally would like to do things to help others be happy and not to suffer. It is not our responsibility to make others happy, but we feel good when others are happy (as long as we don't also resent any unhappiness that we have).

If we have caring feelings for others, then we want things to go well for them. We want them to succeed and be happy. Of course, we all have troubles and have to seek to solve our own problems, but we care about the outcomes for others just as we care about our own outcomes.

If we have caring feelings for others, then we will naturally treat others well. We will treat them as we would like to be treated ourselves, with courtesy and respect and with consideration for their needs and feelings. We will be honest and responsible and treat them fairly and as equals. Treating others well is the compassionate and caring approach in relationships, and it will also maximize your success and your happiness by motivating others to help you to get more of what you want.

Treating others well is the opposite of always looking for ways to take advantage of others. This means telling the truth and being responsible, friendly, and helpful, rather than lying and deceiving, breaking your promises, and demeaning others. You can discover that always treating others well produces a better life for you over the long haul than trying to take things from others inappropriately. Treating others badly results in them distrusting you, refusing to cooperate with you, and trying to take advantage of you, too. (See the Treating Others Well section in my book *Live Wisely, Deeply, and Compassionately* for more.)

We can learn and polish the basics of getting along well with others, if we choose to, including—

- taking others into account when we choose our behaviors
- having a positive attitude toward others
- approaching others in a friendly way
- being happy around others
- giving others basic acceptance
- treating others compassionately
- being kind to others
- treating others with respect and courtesy
- seeing others as basic equals
- refraining from taking advantage of others
- refraining from trying to force others to do what we want
- being understanding with others and understanding others accurately, using accurate empathy
- attending to others' emotional needs
- supporting others' sense of security in the world
- supporting others' sense of self-esteem
- being honest with others
- being responsible
- treating others fairly
- sharing and being generous with others

- bringing appropriate humor to our interactions with others
- communicating effectively with others
- cooperating effectively with others
- controlling one's behavior so as not to harm others
- managing one's emotions so as not to harm others

(See *Living Wisely, Deeply, and Compassionately* (Ebbe, 2023) and the essay Unconditional Love (at www.livewiselydeeply.com under "Living Compassionately" and then "Love") for details about how to embody these desirable qualities.)

Giving Others Basic Acceptance

If you can accept yourself, then you are on the road to truly accepting others as they are, too, for you can see that they have their faults, frailties, and struggles, just as you do, and that they are, for the most part, just as worthy of acceptance as you are. Have compassion for their struggles and their self-rejection, and you can consciously extend your feeling of self-acceptance to them as well.

Accepting someone else means not harming them, criticizing them, putting them down, judgmentally comparing them to others, punishing them, or demeaning them by calling them names. This does not mean accepting all of their behavior—simply that you don't use these methods (harming them, etc.) to try to change them. It would be more fair and less violent to use calm discussion to make clear what you don't like and would like for them to change (and then accept the result or leave!).

You don't have to like everything about someone before accepting him/her. Accepting another person is simply not rejecting or attacking that person. Not rejecting or attacking a person leaves open the possibilities of asking for what you want. It also makes greater communication and cooperation possible. The consequence of not accepting a person is an ineradicable distance between the two of you—unchangeable until you can be more accepting.

Most human beings feel threatened by and therefore reject people who have different beliefs and views from their own, but this can be overcome by understanding those differences better and gaining more security for yourself in life in general. Other peoples' emotions and beliefs are different from yours, because each person is a unique combination of genetics and experience, so each of us sees the world somewhat differently. These differences do not necessarily mean danger or require defending or distancing. You can learn to see the good and the bad about a person without condemning that person (just as we are challenged currently to appreciate both the good and the bad about figures in our history who were also slaveholders).

Understanding more about these differences and why someone else sees the world the way he/she does helps us to feel less threatened. All of us around the world have the same fundamental goals in life—

- survival
- minimal/tolerable physical and emotional pain
- having some pleasure and positive emotions in life
- feeling secure
- feeling good about oneself,
- sex and procreation
- having some gratifying relationships

If we try, we can see how each person is going about seeking these same goals, even people in cultures that look very different from ours.

The most difficult barrier to accepting others is wanting or needing things from them that they do not choose to give, the most common example being when a person marries another person believing (falsely) that he or she will finally be loved or accepted in the way that he/she wants, but finds that this is not happening. The common reaction to this is to keep trying to get the other person to give what is desired, and the usual result is frustration and even violence on both sides and often eventual dissolution of the relationship.

It is not possible to truly accept another person if you feel frustrated about not getting what you want from him or her. The answer to this is to first clarify with the other person that he/she in fact doesn't want to or cannot give what you want, and then to accept that you are not going to get what you want from that person and either enjoy what you can get in that relationship (accepting that you won't get some things you want) or find other sources for what you want or need. Another possibility, of course, is that in the course of dealing with your need and disappointment, you may find that you don't need what you thought you needed as much, or you may discover other sources that allow you not to press your partner to provide that particular thing. Letting go can be difficult, and you may be sad and may need to mourn your loss of hope, but if you conclude sincerely that you are not going to get what you want or need from that person, then it is truly best for you to stop trying to force that person to give what you want, and you will benefit from letting go (and accepting that person as he or she really is).

OVERCOMING BARRIERS TO CARING

Typical barriers to caring for others are—

- ignorance of others
- fear of others
- remembering past disappointments in relationships
- feeling unlovable ourselves
- anger about others not caring
- feeling dislike for others
- seeing others unnecessarily as enemies

Ignorance and Fear of Others

Human beings naturally fear other human beings whom they do not understand and whose behaviors they cannot predict, and it is hard to care for those we fear. Learning about others' individual hopes and characteristics and learning about the coping behaviors of other cultural groups can help dissolve this fear. As noted above, all human beings around the world are striving for the same goals, and in addition to finding this a means of understanding them, we can learn from other individuals and groups as well. You can seek out opportunities to experience those who are different through creating time together (a meal, coffee, an event), and travel gives us a chance to learn about other cultures.

Past Disappointments

If we have had serious disappointments from others in the past for not caring about us, then we will be reluctant to care for others ourselves. To overcome this barrier, we will need the courage to try things that we fear, and we may need to forgive others (and perhaps ourselves as well). Keep your goal in mind as you risk trying to care—to live a happy and comfortable life through caring and relating with others.

Feeling Unlovable Ourselves

If we do not feel lovable ourselves then we will be unable to care for or love others. Our underlying resentment and anger and/or our deep despair will take all of our attention. The way to move forward here is to change our self-image (and self-valuing) to be more accepting, caring, and supportive toward ourselves. For some, this will require outside help (a therapist, a pastor, etc.), but see my book *How To Feel Good About Yourself: Twelve Key Steps To Positive Self-Esteem* for how to work on this yourself.

Anger About Not Being Cared About

In addition to fearing being disappointed again if we have not been cared about appropriately, we may be angry about this and even wish harm to those who have not cared. This anger will prevent you from improving your life and is best processed and forgotten. You will need to be clear about what was done to you, and this can help you to come to a more insightful understanding about why others were unable to care. You will need to be ready to leave that anger behind in favor of positive relating in the present. Some forgiving will probably be needed—of those who didn't care and of yourself for not taking better care of yourself.

Dislike For Others

Caring about others whom we dislike is difficult, but as above, gaining an insightful understanding of the person we dislike can help us relate to him/her even if we continue to dislike certain qualities or behaviors of that person. This requires us to separate the person from his/her behavior and to be able to have different attitudes toward these different elements of the person. Wishing good for someone you dislike or praying for their welfare has been helpful for many in becoming able to relate to others even when the person is disliked.

Seeing Others As Enemies

Going further than dislike, what about actual enemies? As adults, those who use their power over us or who exhibit domination over us are automatically enemies, because they are harming us psychologically or they pose a threat of that harm. Those who harm us physically are automatically enemies because they threaten our existence. We think that we must guard against and seek to defeat enemies, since they are harming us or portend imminent damage to us, so it is easy to engage in the tactics that we grew up with—people expressing their opinions strongly and using their dominance and their ability to harm us to "win" a confrontation and declare victory (nasty words and labels, demeaning us, threatening us). All parents do this to some degree, so all of us see it and learn how to do it.

Key to maintaining our view of others as enemies is our continued ignorance of them. In most cases we don't really know what they think or feel and so don't actually know for sure if they are enemies or not. For those at a distance (those we don't encounter face-to-face ourselves) all we know is what is reported in the news and what others report to us that they have supposedly said or done, but this is usually very limited information. Most of our "enemies," taken as individuals, have a wide variety of opinions (not all exclusively Democratic or Republican opinions), and our whole group of political "enemies" are a bunch of people who individually have many opinions that are different from those of our other enemies, so we should beware of generalizing inappropriately.

Most of those whom we think are our "enemies" are actually "decent" people, which we would know if we actually knew them. Similarity and decency breed alliance, so for someone who loathes Mitch McConnell, seeing him in everyday interaction with staff or family would very likely soften his/her opinion.

Check out the real bases for others' opinions. Some opinions are based on wrong assumptions, and a calm, exploration of facts can help. Many conservative actions are based in a desire to keep things working the way they are currently, and this is a legitimate political stance, but you will miss seeing this if the debate is about whether a specific proposal (such as banning certain books) is itself "right" or "wrong," because no conservative is going to admit in debate that they just want things to stay the same. Many liberal actions are based in empathy or guilt about things being "unfair" in society, which may mean, psychologically, that the liberal person has some doubt about his/her own "right" to all he/she has in life (or has over-empathy, so that every pain of someone else is too much to bear). No liberal person is going to admit that he/she can't stand others' pain and wants us all to change something so there won't be any more pain.

Consider also that you probably have as many or more things in common with a potential enemy than you have differences, and we are all human beings seeking the same goals in life. We are all citizens of the same country, which automatically puts us in the same boat. It may well be that this person is someone you disagree with but of whom you are not really an enemy.

Besides finding out more about supposed enemies, the other key to doing what we can about our political divide is to reassess whether people with opinions different from our own are actually a threat. If they are no threat, then we disagree with them, but they are not enemies. It's harder to talk to enemies, but we can readily talk to those we disagree with, if both of us can keep it civil.

In many cases, it would seem that we should be able to "live and let live." If someone is Jewish and someone else is Catholic, what is the threat (unless one of those groups says they would like to deport those of other faiths or forbid their worship, etc.)? For many of these kinds of disagreements it would seem possible to live side-by-side with those we disagree with if we are comfortable with our own beliefs and if we recognize that the matter is a matter of belief—that there is no factual right or wrong. Do you give people the freedom to live as they wish to live, as long as they are not harming you?

Do you truly give your "opponents" and "enemies" the right to their own opinions, or do you want them to "shut up" and stop bringing your beliefs into question? Can you live with a system where public policy decisions take into account seriously the views of *all* sides? Frankly, to do anything less is to threaten our democracy. If you have to have it your way, then you don't want a democracy. You want a dictatorship of some kind (on the basis of power or religion or ethnic group, etc.).

In our democracy, all should be equal in terms of their influence on our public policy outcomes. If you want to be equal in this sense, then you must give others that right, too. If you want to vanquish the other side, then you don't believe in democracy!

It has become commonplace to say that everyone is biased to some degree about some things, but take care! If "everyone" is biased, then that includes you. If you are biased, too, then you have no basis for asserting, without evidence, that your opinion or belief is more "right" or more "correct" than anyone else's, except that you believe it.

If groups do not interfere with the activities of other groups, there is no reason for them to see each other as enemies. Leftover conceptions and emotions about other countries that are outdated can also cause wars, even though they "should" not do so.

If we look a carefully at the situation, there is no good reason for us to view Russia as a mortal enemy now (with the single exception of persons in leadership whose feelings are coming from the past and no longer apply). When Communism was young and aggressive and seeking to convert the world, by fair means or foul, we had some reason to fear, particularly after Russia acquired a huge stockpile of nuclear weapons and intercontinental ballistic missiles, but now, following the "fall" of the USSR and of Communism, Russia does not seem to have much motivation to harm us or take over our country (except for their unfounded fear of us). It is quite certain that ordinary Russians do not want to take over the U.S., just as ordinary Americans have no interest in taking over or "defeating" Russia. Russia does want to have a buffer of countries between it and NATO (one of them being Ukraine), but that is because they fear us and NATO (as well as because the grandiosity of Mr. Putin seems to require it). We claim that they have no reason to fear us (right?), and as far as I know, the U.S. does not want to eliminate or take over Russia. We just want to protect ourselves, right?

So here we have a good example of a dangerous and perhaps totally unnecessary view of an enemy and a situation, which could possibly lead to nuclear war, all because of ignorant fears. They fear us unnecessarily, and we fear them unnecessarily. Wouldn't it be wise to reconsider the whole antipathy between Russia and the U.S.? Who, if anyone, really wants war or to "take over" the other? We cannot feel safe of we assume that because we grew up fearing Russia, we should continue to do so until the day we die. In fact, doesn't Russia have more to fear from China than from the U.S.? Perhaps Russia should join in with the U.S. in a mutual defense treaty!

Similarly with China. There is no more reason for China to fear us than for us to fear it, is there? We don't want to take over China (we just want to protect ourselves, right?), and China doesn't want to take over the world. The U.S., Russia, and China are too huge to manage for anyone who did take them over, which convinces me that no one will try (as long as there are none in China's ruling class who actually think they should fear the U.S.).

There is special danger to many when leaders are over-sensitive to threat and domination, since they are then more likely engage in violence or war, either against their own people (citizens who do not accept their special status as leaders) or against other groups (either because of harm or threat of harm or by using other groups as scapegoats or stand-ins for those toward whom they are actually angry).

What can you do to be more accurate in identifying actual enemies? Think for yourself. Just because someone else is upset about something doesn't mean that there is good reason for them to be upset or good reason for you to be upset.

Find out as much as you can about "the facts." Look to various media and other sources of opinion, not just to one source.

Interact with some people whose opinions are different from yours. Size them up as people, not just opinions. Find out what they actually "mean" when they express their opinions. Find out the real reasons why they are upset about something or want to change something.

Search within yourself for why a difference of opinion seems like a threat to you. Is it really a threat or only an arousing invitation to have an argument? What do you actually believe?

Examine yourself for resentment or over-sensitivity due to your childhood experiences of harm or humiliation, so that you can see the behavior of others more clearly (often perceiving their vulnerability, weakness, and aggressive or dominating behavior as being due to their own insecurity and their experience of harm or humiliation), so that you can empathize with them and seek joining solutions rather than conflict.

Redefine "enemy." If you feel that someone is an enemy, ask yourself why? Work on your own confidence in your opinions and positions until you can allow others to have theirs without you feeling threatened by that. Give "live and let live" a chance.

Before thinking of someone as an enemy, think about the ways in which he/she has things in common with you. You may have many more things in common, as citizens and persons, than you have differences of opinion, and this may mean that you disagree but are not really enemies.

Before you speak, ask yourself if you are giving others the rights you want for yourself. If we are all equals, then we all have the same right to have and express those opinions.

Commit yourself to supporting a system of government in which all opinions are heard (with appropriate respect) and then debated until an appropriate compromise is reached. Say that to others who treat you like an enemy!

DEVELOPING CARING ABILITIES

In order to care effectively for others and to be able to lessen their suffering, it is important that we understand their feelings and needs. This is most effectively done through our ability to empathize with them (understand their experience through observation without direct communication). See my book *Live Wisely, Deeply, and Compassionately* or my article on empathy on the website www.livewiselydeeply.com under Human Functioning/Coping.

EXPANDING OUR CIRCLE OF CARING

We are adapted to small groups, like villages, and our feelings center on people we know. Evolution has not yet had time to help us get better at relating with bigger groups. So, it is not easy to expand to the whole world of human beings concepts that we learn in our small groups, like caring for others. It's easy and natural to care for everyone in our families, and we can fairly readily expand this to a small village, but the world?! Normally we have feelings for individuals that we have direct contact with, but what about those we will never encounter?

Assuming that you want to have a caring attitude toward all people, imagine the feeling of caring that you have for your loved ones, and then hold that feeling and think of people in China or India or Ireland and continue to feel that same caring feeling while you contemplate all those people who are equal human beings to yourself. Imagine their lives including some suffering, just like yours, and feel your hope that their suffering might be decreased. Imagine that you are radiating your caring to all of them. They deserve the kind of positive warmth and well-wishing in their lives that you do and that all those that you love do.

Think of caring as you conceive of it, perhaps as an aura or bubble around you, and imagine that aura or bubble getting bigger until it includes people other than your loved ones. It can get big enough to include all human beings.

We each "deserve" all the good things in life that are available to all, including caring and love, and we each can treat others with positive warmth and good wishes that express the caring within us.

The world's major religions all teach having care and compassion for everyone. You may benefit from exploring how this is expressed in religions other than your own, and if it helps your caring attitude to model it after a figure dear to your heart, such as Jesus for Christians or Buddha for Buddhists, then do it.

Buddhism and Christian mysticism include spiritual practices that can help us be more aware of our caring and compassion and focus it outward as well as inward. Buddhist mantras for meditation are an example (such as "May I grow in love and may my love reach out to others and lessen their suffering just a little").

Fear and ignorance are the enemies of equality and caring. If we fear someone, it is harder to care about him/her, and this fear most often comes from our ignorance about him/her that causes us to be unable to see his/her suffering and deservingness. We are all in the same boat on this earth. Some of us have the good fortune of being in much better economic conditions than others, and we did nothing to be in this position and do not "deserve" being in this condition any more than any other person in the universe.

We can transcend our tribal instincts if we attend to our attitudes. We need and always will need our own family circles of love, but if we view others as having the same struggles that we do and as being just as needful of support and being treated well as we do, we can expand our circles of caring to include the world.

The following affirmation can help. Try reading it over every morning before you get up.

"I look forward to moving through today with a caring attitude toward everyone, because I feel happiest myself when I live with this warm and affectionate feeling and attitude. I will view myself and others compassionately, and I will accept all of us as the wonderful though imperfect persons that we are. I will be aware of my own barriers to being more caring and will serenely move beyond them as I can. I will spread warmth and good feeling by approaching others positively and by being the one to take the first step in establishing connections with them.

I will see others as sources of good feelings and pleasant experiences for me, and I will enjoy the warmth and affection that can exist in every interaction. I will see the humanness in each individual, just as I see it in myself, for we are all part of one big human family. I will appreciate that we all have the same emotional possibilities and have the same basic goals in life, which makes it easier to bring positivity to each of our interactions.

I will do what I can to reduce the suffering of everyone I meet, and I will hope for happiness and good things for each person."

SPECIFIC POPULATIONS

As our culture changes over time, gender roles and how we parent children also change. These changes are painful for many, since they upend how many believe that they "should" be living. All who are affected deserve our informed caring.

The Position of the Marginalized and Disadvantaged

People who look different from the majority continue to encounter prejudice and unfairness in our society—particularly Blacks, (East) Indians, and Asians. Many Muslims encounter religious prejudice. Efforts have been made to use existing laws to overcome prejudicial activities (particularly regarding access to college or financial opportunities), but even positive outcomes of these lawsuits do not change the hearts of those who are prejudiced. There are discussions currently of financial reparations for descendants of slaves in this country. (I think that reparations could have some value symbolically but would unleash so much negative backlash in society (like canceling student loan debt has) that they would fail in their objective, and I doubt that the money itself would be used in ways that would change the socioeconomic position of those receiving it.)

Those who are prejudiced cling to prejudices that enhance their own status, thus revealing that they do not feel valuable without being able to point to groups who they can claim are less valuable than themselves. (This applies even among Blacks with regard to color gradation used to establish status.) It is pointless and even cruel to take engrained status away from those who need it, so the larger answer to prejudice must be greater equality and a lessening of status concerns. Every citizen should be able to feel valued and secure in that value regardless of external characteristics or relative status. This is a matter of attitude. All of us should move toward giving up the status positions that we use to bolster our sense of value and utilize the attitudes described in this section instead, so that *know* that we are valuable and so that being an equal part of the larger group is enough to feel good about ourselves. *I will lead in this attitude change and will ensure (as far as I can) that no government actions occur that disadvantage any groups of citizens.*

The Position of Women

Across history, cultures have handled the differences between men and women in various ways, many of them making men higher status and many of them restricting women to roles in homemaking and childrearing. From an economic standpoint, these arrangements may have been valuable when such narrow focus and patriarchal dominance were actually related to some degree to survival of the group, but in this era, this is not necessary. In order to maintain social order and defend the country it is not necessary for men to dominate women or to have more rights than women, and it is not necessary for women to only bear children and organize the home. It is feasible now for things to be more equal.

Another existential problem for women is the physical strength superiority of men, which men, particularly given their biological predisposition to violence (to protect the group), can always use to get their way with women (sex or submission of one sort or another). *I will encourage attitudes of equality between men and women, and I will highlight the frequent use of violence against women by men so that we can establish a stronger norm against this.* This is not to deny the true differences which do exist between the sexes, particularly around the instinct of men to protect by fighting and the instinct of women to nurture through safety and love, but men and women can all master the rudiments of both kinds of roles so that they can perform both as needed. And regardless of the roles we decide on, all citizens should treat all other citizens with respect and courtesy at all times.

We have made significant progress in improving women's position over the lasts fifty years, seeing now that women can be effective bosses and men can be homemakers. In fact, our transition from being a manufacturing society to being a service society has put men at a disadvantage, as illustrated by increasing suicide rates in men and the fact that more women go to college than men. This will all even out over time, but right now it is still painful for many.

A key disadvantage for women in both being homemakers and having work careers is that being home to do the very important job of raising children for their first (six?) years means that when re-entering the work force, these women have less work experience in their resumes and are therefore less likely to be hired than men of the same age with more years of experience. *I will propose that women who have been out of the work force for at least several (six?) years will be, by law, given compensatory experience credit by people doing hiring.* The amount of this credit will be a matter of debate to be settled by Congress. This will probably seem unfair to some men, but some adjustment like this is the only way not to have important early childrearing be a lifelong disadvantage for those women who undertake it (and who want another career for themselves). *This credit would be available as well to men who are doing the childrearing.*

Other Opinions
We've gone far enough in equalizing opportunity for men and women. You will penalize companies if you force them to take as part of their work force people who are less qualified to do the jobs.

#MeToo
The increasing willingness of women (and some men) to make public how they have been sexually abused (harassed or assaulted) is to be supported. It is long overdue. However, this makes it even more important to address the dilemma of whether to believe all things that are reported in this way. Uncertainty about believing claims of sexual abuse has resulted over past decades in judicial stalemates because of the "she said—he said" nature of many of these cases (unless there is an unusual amount of actual evidence in addition to the accusation itself). Now that the dam has broken regarding the abused giving this information, there is a strong tendency to believe all accusations, almost to make up for women not being believed in the past. We should take all accusations seriously,

but we will have to accept that without corroboration, many accusations will not result in punishment under our legal system. We have a tendency to "rush to judgment" on emotional bases only, without giving any credence to an accused persons rejoinder. I believe everyone deserves an appropriate amount of due process before legal punishments, and we should take care that non-legal punishments (being fired, publicly humiliated, being cancelled, etc.) are not too excessive, since they may well be unfair. Don't forget that the mob could unfairly turn against you someday.

Other Opinions
The only way to even up the score is for some men to be unfairly punished. Get used to it. Cancel culture, though crude and unfair, does put abusers on notice about what may happen to them, and this is positive.

The Position of Men
While men may have benefited for centuries from patriarchal arrangements in society, the times are changing, and young men in particular are showing alarming signs of dysfunction. Women fill the majority of college seats now, are more independent than ever before, and are more choosy about mates. The desired image of men is changing from an emphasis on strength and competition to a more egalitarian role in the family and a more equalitarian role in service and financial jobs. Young men are confused about who they are supposed to be, as they are no longer rewarded for physical violence or for being "the lord of the house." Through the course of evolution, strength and fighting have been the favored characteristics for men (producing the most surviving children), and now we are asking them to go against whatever elements of that role are inbred in them.

This is one element that contributed to the Jan. 6 riot in Washington, D.C.—men who feel left behind and without clear career paths. *I will seek ways to model and legitimize for men the new roles expected of them and will seek to develop and fund a vast network across the country of technical schools to make career preparation easier for men (and the women who might favor those careers). I will also encourage apprenticeship approaches to hiring by businesses.* (Note that we are not hoping that men will no longer be strong but that they will expand their role capacities beyond strength to include more nurturance and emotion management.)

Other Opinions

Men will never change, and the result of this feminization of society will ultimately be that our country will be taken over by some society that still believes that men should be men. Men who cannot lead and dominate their families are not really men, and women who want complete equality will be sorry with whatever male substitutes that we produce.

The Position of Children

Young adults have a more complex world to face than we did when we were children, since there are so many more opportunities, things are much more interconnected, and we are all much more interdependent. There is no guarantee that one's career choice won't disappear as a casualty of economic growth, and there is little security in any job. We have also done many of our children a disservice by moving them to urban and suburban settings where they have little contact with nature (local parks don't count) and little opportunity to explore the world around them since we fear (falsely) that they can be molested or kidnapped at any time.

Children also face anonymous competition (alone and without potential support from their parents) on the internet where they are bombarded with the immature bragging and false boasting of supposed peers with a jaundiced, immature view of what is important in life (looking better, being "above" others) as well as attacks by mean-spirited others.

Many children these days think that their lives are supposed to be desperate efforts to get into the best schools and obtain the highest paying jobs (by looking good and achieving an image that is not really themselves), so it is no wonder that the suicide rate in children has ballooned. Parents must look deep into themselves to figure out what is really important in life and then to give their children those values (hopefully, that other people are important and valuable and that finding fulfillment in life is more important than getting more money).

We need to give our kids more confidence in their ability to navigate the world and exist side by side with others. Lessons in ballet and participation in local youth sports (where they too often learn that winning is everything or that everyone gets a trophy) are not enough. Parents must be involved sufficiently in the lives of their children that they can share their wisdom at appropriate points and their support as needed. Criticizing and urging children to "buck up" or just work harder (or just telling them that everything will be all right no matter how badly they feel) are not what kids need. Parents must be loving consultants, and few know how to do this in a way that is supportive and not threatening.

I will support activities that enable children to learn about the big world (live for a summer with a family in another part of the country; summer camps to acquaint children with the rest of the world; etc.) and that help children to have good self-esteem (especially a positive view of themselves and the ability to properly evaluate any criticism or rejection they encounter). I will also support high school curricula that give training regarding lifetime management of finances, understanding taxes, how to stay healthy, how to have a good marriage, how to raise healthy children, etc.), as well as making good parenting education available in every community.

Other Opinions
Kids will always adjust to whatever they encounter. We don't have to go farther into cossetting them by special camps to learn about the world—they get that when they are told to move out or pay rent.

The Position of Non-Gender-Conforming Citizens
It is quite amazing how much more accepting of gay persons our society has become over the last thirty years. Transgender and other non-gender-conforming persons have benefited a bit from this but have a long way to go to be truly accepted in society. A person not identifying with his/her birth-assigned gender may be hard for some people to understand, but professionally as a psychologist, I assure you that gender dysphoria is usually sincere and painful. *They will be treated equally and just as well as any other citizen under my administration—with respect and courtesy and with just as much access to services as anyone else would have.*

In households where the notion of children being gay or trans from birth is accepted, I believe there have been too many cases of noticing a behavior (a biological male child playing with dolls) and concluding that they should immediately encourage stereotypical female behaviors in that child. As a psychologist I know that children have widespread interests and try out many possible behaviors, so it is unwise to narrow down their possibilities too early. It is much better to give children free rein and wait until adolescence to see which way they are trending in general. For this reason, unless it is quite certain over a period of years that a child's inclination is one way or another (and there are some such clear cases), it is unwise to begin supportive medical treatments (hormones, surgery) until late adolescence. Mental health professionals with experience in this area can assist in advising parents whether or not to be actively supportive of cross-gender behavior.

In regard to the current controversy over competition in women's sports events by persons who were biologically male but now identify as female, I do not believe that this is fair, unless the individual had puberty-blocking medications throughout adolescence *and* has the individual review and OK of the authority governing the particular sport (perhaps including hormone testing). It is not appropriate for persons who are systematically stronger and larger on a hormonal basis to compete in this way, even though we can be sympathetic to those who end up in this situation and are blocked from competing.

Other Opinions

God has assigned our sex and our sexual preference (straight, gay, etc.), and sex and gender are the same thing. Any deviation from this is a mistake and sinful. Families suffer greatly from a member going against this reality.

ENCOURAGING TRUTH IN GOVERNMENT

Truth has taken quite a beating over the last twenty years, as "the facts" have gotten more and more complex, and many citizens have almost given up trying to understand what is true and what is not. Politicians, cable news, and social media have augmented this trend by over-simplifying or outright lying without suffering any consequences. Mr. Trump was a great one for over-simplifying and sloganning, thereby giving us many distortions that he hoped we would believe. (He may maintain that he really believes what he says, exactly as he says it, but I maintain that he knows when he is distorting. Note how careful he was prior to Jan. 6 not to directly incite riot.)

I maintain that there is such a thing as truth, and although the truth about many things may be complex and we may not have all the facts at our disposal to be sure of our conclusions, we still have a duty, with regard to ourselves and our fellow citizens, to do our best to understand things and to get as close to the truth as we can, even when we don't like what we are finding. *I will always try to adhere to the truth in what I say to everyone, and as noted above, I will use the web to send you explanations that are accurate and make sense.*

In philosophy, the "post-modernist" movement gave us something of value by pointing out how many things that we take to be true are actually constructed by ourselves to make them seem like these truths are not just opinion but are based in some other (non-human) set of facts or based in some external (non-human) authority (e.g., democracy is the best form of government; the U.S. is the best country in the world; the U.S. is a Christian country). However, some took this too far by claiming that there was no such thing as truth. I maintain that truth is still a useful concept, as long as we recognize the limits of our knowledge and stay alert to our tendency to attribute greater "truth-value" to the things we want to believe. Things can be "as true as the limits of our human knowledge can make them, with our personal biases removed," and these are still useful truths (e.g., the U.S. is the country that is richest in material terms and the first to have a written, democratic constitution).

I believe that basing our lives and our decisions in things that are as true as we can get them to be results in better lives for us and our loved ones, even though believing anything we want to believe (true or not) can feel better!

Other Opinions

Who are you to challenge our view of what is true? We can find experts to support our side just as you have them on your side. There is no such thing as truth, so give up trying for truth and join the rest of us in our emotional and admittedly untruthful battle for hearts and minds.

HONESTY

In order to work together effectively and amicably, we must be able to trust each other, and the key to trust is honesty. You are no doubt aware of politicians who will say whatever they think people would like to hear at the moment, even if they themselves don't even believe it, with little commitment to carrying out what they have promised if elected. I will always reveal my motives for every proposal, and I will always say what I mean (clearly and unambiguously) and mean what I say. If my views change on a topic, I will let you know and tell you why.

Part of the "prevailing wisdom" regarding elections is that one must minimize offending anyone, because that would arouse single-issue voters to vote against one. This results in candidates always speaking vaguely and avoiding specifics, so that you don't really know whether to vote for them or not. I will always tell you what I think. Candidates don't reveal themselves to you because they want you to vote for them regardless of their views and qualifications (i.e., regardless of how you would be impacted if they were elected). This is a recipe for electing the wrong people! In return for getting the full information about me, I ask you to look at the total of my positions when you judge my candidacy. Don't just reject me because you disagree with one or two of my positions. You will probably never know what the other candidates' positions are on those issues anyway!

From my observations, there are many candidates who apparently believe that people are honest only when it is to their advantage and that lying is OK if it helps you get what you want. I believe that we should be honest with each other because it makes for a better life for us all, and because we care about each other. "Let the buyer beware" is a cheap way of sellers evading responsibility for being dishonest. I believe that a seller should have the honesty and the caring about the buyer to tell the buyer both the pros and the cons of the product.

Also, exaggeration is used frequently by politicians, apparently to make things seem simple and to vilify the other side. Doing this is dishonest. Statements on policy issues should explain the reasons for one's position *and* the reasons for other positions as well.

POLITICAL SPEECH

While the Constitution guarantees the right of citizens to voice their opinions on political matters without fear of reprisal, in my view it is inappropriate that the Supreme Court has equated political contributions and speech (and given corporations a right to make unlimited political contributions). Corporations should not be able to make unlimited campaign contributions, and money is not speech! The results have been to boost the money wasted on elections (non-educational efforts to sway voters) and to legitimate and increase the self-serving efforts in the media by all groups to deceive citizens, through lying or subterfuge. Almost all of current political advertising is done in this way. Unions, corporations, PACs, and political parties tend to construct their supposedly protected expressions for maximum influence value by using misstatements, misleading statements, innuendo, outright lies, and omission of key facts. Attempts to influence others by organizations should be subject to the misdemeanor penalties described below, because this lying is done purposely and could easily be corrected. (Individual citizens may sometimes attempt to influence the opinions of others by using false statements, but their power to influence on an individual basis is limited enough, except of course for multimillionaires, that this can be tolerated for the sake of protecting their fundamental right of expression.)

I will work to make clear through legislation that organizations are not citizens. On the other hand, organizations do have a right to express themselves and their desires, as long as it is done truthfully or with desire primarily to educate. The country might be better off if only individuals could contribute to political parties and candidates (up to a one million dollar limit!), while still allowing corporations and other groups to express their opinions.

I will also institute a fact-checking arm of the federal government which will point out the deception efforts and provide corrections on-line to as much of this advertising as possible. This effort will be fair to all, and complaints concerning its own bias will be accepted and investigated. I will personally monitor this effort.

Other Opinions

I deserve my truth, just as you do. You can't tell me I'm lying. My rights to free speech guarantee that I can say whatever I want. The campaign competition through money is simply one way to show who is preferred.

LYING BY CANDIDATES AND ELECTED OFFICIALS

Misrepresentation by office holders is common, as they attempt to get elected by lying or withholding information about themselves or their plans if elected. This is lying, either by misrepresentation or by omission, and I will seek to make doing so a misdemeanor (when they actually know that what they are saying is false or misleading). Of course we all have free speech rights, including candidates, but speech has consequences. Already it is a crime to falsely cause a panic or threaten someone's life. It is equally important not to elect liars or people who know so little that they can't help but lie!

I will seek to make such misrepresentation and lying a misdemeanor crime. Office holders can have their own opinions and can voice them publicly if they qualify them as their opinions (e.g., "I think...," "I believe...," "In my opinion...," etc.), but to purposely give partial, misleading information to sway voters should be illegal. Thus, in communicating about weapons of mass destruction, if the President says "Nation A has weapons of mass destruction" (instead of "According to our best assessment of the current data, though it is still somewhat uncertain, we believe that Nation A has weapons of mass destruction," unless there is irrefutable proof that Nation A does in fact have those weapons, it would be a misdemeanor.

I will set up an organization to identify the misrepresentations and outright lies of candidates (including myself!), office holders, and supporters of candidates and to make them readily available to the public (similar to current fact-checking organizations). This organization will be scrupulously fair in its investigations and will develop a good reputation, much as the GAO now has.

I will also seek to make it mandatory in public information (like ads on TV) that each candidate or speaker present both sides of issues, rather than only their own and how they would like things to be.

I understand that some citizens will discount my candidacy because of my stand about lying, because they believe that no one can know the truth and therefore everyone should be able to lie without cost, or they believe that no system can be fair in determining whether someone has lied. I can only say that the degree of truthfulness of any statement can be assessed, at least with reference to what we know about the subject, and that there are many people in our society who can do that in a fair way, because they are able to set aside their own preferences for the sake of truth. You may not know any of these people, but I do.

Other Opinions

It is natural to human beings to exaggerate, and most lying is white lying, so you're making way to big a deal out of this. You'll never be able to convict anyone of intentional lying, since you can't prove what's in a person's mind, and you can't require a level of knowledge adequate to say that a person "should have known" or "could readily have known" that he/she was lying, because that would get into infringing the free speech of those who are not capable of that knowledge. Nice try, but no cigar.

SOCIAL MEDIA

Social media companies are private companies but have become so large and play such a large role in the lives of many citizens that they require government regulation, particularly in terms of somehow policing the efforts by some individuals and groups to harm other internet users (bullying, lying to change voters' minds, pretending to be other than who they actually are). We must both prevent speech intended to harm while protecting political speech and encouraging speech in general. Government will have to establish guidelines to protect the public from purposive harm, since we will never be satisfied with the standards that these private companies will establish to police themselves. This will be difficult, since some harmful speech will be claimed to be simply factual, but we must struggle with this ethical issue. (See Lying by Candidates and Elected Officials above for more.) In the end, users must be responsible for what they allow into their brains. If they are being harmed and know it, they may simply have to stop using that media.

One thing that could be done to reconcile the needs of different populations of internet users would be to have, in every open forum on the internet, separate tracks for adults and children and separate tracks for (1) discussion aimed at information-sharing, learning, and growing and (2) self-expression that employs a considerable amount of swearing, name-calling, and other degrading speech, threats, slander, bullying, etc. This way we could accommodate more speech and not have to "censor" at least the swearing, etc. Another procedure would be to have everyone identify each post as either "opinion" or "fact-based claim," and having a fact-based claim would require that at least one supposed fact would be included. This could be checked to some degree by an algorithm, but even if some things included as "fact" were not facts, this procedure would make everyone a little more conscious of the difference between opinion (99 percent of what is posted on the internet) and fact-based argument. We should probably also have time limits (such as one day) for removal of dangerous speech by the forum (speech that could cause imminent harm), after which the forum is fined for each further day that it takes to remove the post. The decisions regarding "imminent harm" would sometimes be difficult – e.g, would falsehoods urging people not to get an approved vaccine be a cause of imminent harm? (In my opinion, reasoned arguments based on some data which suggest that people might not wish to get this vaccine would not be considered to be a cause of harm. Similarly, reasoned arguments from data claiming that vaccines were not effective would not automatically be considered a cause of harm.)

See "Ad Fontes" for a company that rates bias of media outlets.

Other Opinions
People are responsible for what they choose to read, and if they read things that cause them depression or even suicide, that is still their responsibility. Some people can't express themselves without swearing or stretching the truth, and they should still be able to post without restriction.

OUR TWO-PARTY SYSTEM

Our two-party system is not serving us well, though it may have done so in our country's early history. The struggle between Democrats and Republicans for power is responsible for much of our government gridlock and for the atmosphere of distrust and fighting that pervades our society. Our two parties have polarized into archetypal conservative vs. liberal groups which now fight about that general difference ("progress" vs. tradition), using current issues as touchstones for the right vs. left struggle (abortion, immigration, etc.), rather than debating issues on their actual merits. The two major parties have built into the system many ways which are to their advantage, and we should dismantle some of that advantage (which makes third parties or write-in voting much more difficult).

We also need to reconceptualize our thinking about political groupings in our society, since registered Republicans and Democrats each around only thirty percent of eligible voters now, while that amorphous group of "independents" accounts for forty percent! The crucial point here is that the two major parties do not represent the totality of the American electorate—not even close. We need a way for the will of more individual Americans to enter the process, rather than pretending that only sixty percent (Democrats and Republicans) should be represented. It is natural for people to group together with others who have similar values and ideas, but the goal should be more open consideration of all ideas rather than narrowing down to only two.

A further problem is the change that our two parties have made toward election by popularity rather than election by competence or election by platform. The Republican party has not even had a platform (a statement of what they would like to do for the country) for the last few elections! Every political group should be challenged to tell you, the voter, what its vision is for the country. What would it like to do for businesses *and* for workers? What role would it like to see religion play in our country?

While multiparty systems have their drawbacks as well, *I will encourage the growth of other parties and seek to curtail the power of the current two parties, including seeking legislation to outlaw the practice of parties telling their members how they "should" or "must" vote on bills before Congress (and prohibiting parties from "punishing" members who do not vote with the party).* This would result in more varied opinions about those bills and greater creativity in solving problems. *I will also encourage voters who would like to see change to register as independent rather than as either Democrat or Republican.*

It is natural for human beings to want to protect themselves and their means of surviving and living from anything threatening, but we have created a false dichotomy regarding approaches to improving our country. Every individual has a greater variety of thoughts about how they would like to see the country operate than our two parties do. Legislators flock together to have more power than any one individual could have, but unfortunately this emphasis on power leads to a single opinion, conflict, and gridlock. A better way for government to operate is to seek understanding of other positions and then be willing to seek the best compromise possible (the one that benefits the most citizens and disadvantages the fewest citizens) and then live with that compromise, rather than waiting until their own group is in the majority and can try to force everyone else to live like they think best.

We can have some compassion for our legislators, who have a hard job trying to understand complex issues and stay in touch with their constituents needs and beliefs. Being away from their homes (in Washington), they naturally associate with others in their same boat and tend to do that more with those who see the world as they do rather than with those who are different. This naturally leads to the development of parties, in hopes of having enough power to get things done. It's an insightful legislator who can know his own beliefs clearly and still understand and accept the needs and beliefs of others!

Parties tend to use their power over members to control the outcomes of voting on bills and to make those outcomes more certain or predictable. Often parties won't even allow a bill to be voted on unless they know they can win (by having already counted up the votes they can count on). *The alternative that I propose is for every representative and senator to vote as they think best for their constituency and best for the country and then see how the vote comes out, since I believe that everyone "voting their consciences" creates the most accurate representation of the will of the people.* There will be resistance to this idea from those who want to "win" rather than ascertain the will of the people. (Usually the references to "the American people" by politicians really means "the people that agree with me" and not the will of the people as a whole.) Having Congresspersons vote independently of party will make the outcomes of votes less predictable (but more exciting). Having votes on every bill will take more time, but the benefit of not having the two parties in control will outweigh this cost.

A convincing argument can be made that anyone who tries to control the vote of a representative or senator, beyond encouraging that representative or senator to speak his/her own mind about the issue at hand, is by doing that interfering with democracy, because it is the will of the voters that we should be seeking, not the will of anyone else. A representative or senator who tries to change the vote of another representative or senator is distorting democracy (unless he/she is pointing out a way in which the one he/she is speaking to can represent his/her own constituency even better). Every American should speak up about what he/she wants from government (about every issue), but trying to manipulate the votes and views of other Americans distorts the basic will of the people. Think about whether you believe in democracy (democracy as in every vote counts, people should vote independently, and the majority vote wins OR democracy as people giving up their individual votes to someone who knows better or to a larger group which can have greater influence than they can). Again, we need more diversity of opinions in our deliberations, rather than narrowing them down to only two.

I don't think that I should be called a "third-party" candidate, since I don't think being in a party is a good thing for a president. Besides a way of gathering power in numbers, parties are an excuse for voters not to have to get to know candidates. Parties come up with some simple slogans and emotional ideas that give cues to voters on how to vote without really educating them about any of the issues. Right now, many voters would side with the Democrats if they strongly believed that our society should reduce inequality, even if they know nothing about other stands that the party takes or how it would go about reducing inequality (or the national debt). Similarly, right now, many voters would side with the Republican party if they thought that society was changing too fast and that immigrants were one of the causes of the changing, regardless of any other stands that the party takes or what it would do to slow down change.

I am telling you how I view all of the problems by means of this platform. You will not agree with all of my views and proposals, but you must decide, on balance, whether I am a better candidate in your eyes than the other candidates. The problem with this it that you don't know what the stands of the other candidates are or what they would do. They talk in generalities which don't tell you very much, and most of that is on emotional issues (abortion, minimum wage, illegal immigration) where they want you to side with them for their emotional take on that issue without telling you what they would or could actually do about it. Besides Bernie Sanders and Elizabeth Warren, has any Democratic candidate told you how he/she will reduce inequality? Has any Republican candidate told you what they would actually do about immigration at our southern border? Would they actually stop all immigration? Would they spend enough to staff enough immigration workers at the border to process all those immigrants? You don't know (and neither do they). (See the section "The Wall" in my platform for more.)

A related issue is the matter of primary elections to select candidates who will be on the actual election ballot. Currently these primaries are dominated by the extremes of both major parties, since more of them will participate in these primary elections than will more moderate party members. This results in having more extreme candidates in the actual election. To further reduce the power of the two major parties, *I support having open primaries in which all candidates (including those of both major parties) are on a single ballot, and the top vote-getters are on the actual election ballot.* (The number of those to be on the actual election ballot would be decided by each state.)

Readers might take note that there are at least two groups in the country who are also working to reduce the power of the two major parties—the Forward Party and more recently the No Labels group. Check out their websites. (It is probably more accurate not to call them "parties," since they both want us to move away from party affiliations.)

Other Opinions
To let senators and representatives vote as they see fit would lead to chaos. How would we know whether we can win or not before a vote? How would we have any power? The parties do useful work in combining the views of their members into one view which can then be promoted by all. The "will of the people" is expressed in electing people, and those people who are elected then have complete freedom to do whatever they want to.

ACCEPTING COMPROMISE AS THE NORM FOR OUR DEMOCRACY

Democracy is ideally a system of gathering the equally valuable input from all citizens and then fashioning the best solutions possible at the moment for each and every problem. Democracy should not be about who can "win" and force everyone else to do as they direct; it must be about making the best compromises possible on every issue. The current emphasis on winning leads to the parties putting off even voting on needed proposals if they cannot win at that moment, which leads to ineffective and then erratic government as they overturn previous "wins" by the other side. I will work for effective and acceptable compromises for all of our problems. This will mean some citizens will have to give up their crusades to force their moral beliefs and attitudes on everyone else. (I believe now that there is more compromising going on in Congress than I realized some months ago, which is all to the good, but more can be done in this regard, and I will champion it, as well as highlight to the public the work of those in Congress who are doing their best to compromise.)

Our citizens are too focused on winning and too little focused on getting things done. In a diverse country, there will always be opposing views, each with some justification for those views (some more, some less), and this points us in the direction of seeking the most effective compromises on most issues. It is fine for everyone to state their beliefs and principles, but these positions vary in their pros and cons, and we must incorporate the best from each of them in our effective compromises. Ideological purity leads us toward winner-take-all government that lurches forward through time constantly changing direction and doubling back on itself as political parties gain and lose power. I will encourage respectful, well thought out arguments on issues, rather than mutual insults and purposeful exaggeration. Fighting makes a good draw on TV, but it is not the best way to make decisions or to educate voters. Fighting and trying to "win" over the other side leads simply to more anger and hatred. (Compromise is not dead in D.C. The Bipartisan Policy Center brings Congresspersons together to work on possible compromises out of the media spotlight and facilitates home visits between Republican and Democrat Congresspersons! The Friends Council on National Legislation (Quaker) also provides private work space and facilitation for efforts toward compromise.)

As an example of compromise, it seems to me that recent positions expressed on abortion (restricting abortion after two trimesters or fifteen weeks, with exceptions for rape, incest, and the life of the mother) represent an effective compromise. Neither side gets all it wants, but both sides get something significant. Going beyond this, to outlawing abortion totally (or removing all restrictions on abortion), moves away from this compromise to attempt an ideological "win" and will engender much more anger and conflict.

The process for effective and amicable compromise is not complicated.

(1) Understand what all sides (blocs and individuals) want. This may be something concrete but more often is related to something emotional. This reflects deep visions of our future country, which help to make sense of current requests/demands (viz., the current "culture wars"). Effective compromise is not just a trade-off negotiation but a quest to find ways to satisfy all sides and to have all sides feel heard and taken into account.

(2) Offer possible compromises that will benefit everyone to some extent. The common strategy in negotiating of asking for too much, expecting to then have "bargaining room" just slows the process greatly. It helps to establish trust to offer compromises that one would accept that very day, with no need for "bargaining down" (which is by definition a demeaning process). This "up-frontness" requires having everyone's best interest at heart (and believing that everyone else has your best interests at heart) rather than trying to get as much for only one group as one can. This kind of cooperative compromise work is possible if you care, even a little, about the welfare of other citizens, as well as the welfare of your own group. If you don't care about the welfare of other citizens, then you are a drag on the processes that make for a happy, cooperative society. You may say, "but that's how people are—trying to get our own way; we're all that way," and I say "no, everyone isn't that way, and it would be a happier and more pleasant country if people who did care about their fellow citizens

and about fairness in government would step up to the plate, say so, and vote accordingly!

(3) Accept satisfactory compromises with a good heart, rather than planning already on ways to get more of your way in the future. Bring up even better compromises as economics or culture changes make them possible.

Other Opinions
It is the American way to fight for what you want, and Americans want the best fighter to lead them. There's nothing like a speech vilifying the other side to bring people together! Getting the better of your adversary in a negotiation is a thrill just like killing a deer when you go hunting.

LIVING WITH COMPROMISE

If we compromise, none us may get exactly what we want. The price of compromise, therefore, is living with what is not exactly what we want but seems to everyone to be the most effective and fair solution at the present time. You must believe that this will produce better outcomes for you (and everyone else) over the long haul, rather than fighting all the time to get just what you want when that would be to the disadvantage of other citizens (the "other side" who won't vote for your way). You must ultimately decide which way you want the country to function.

Other Opinions
It is the American way to strive for what you want, and naturally all of us want things to be the way we want them to be. So, it would be un-American to give up on your desires and compromise. If people would just agree to see things our way, things would be so much better for the country.

TAXES, A BALANCED BUDGET, GOVERNMENT BORROWING, AND THE NATIONAL DEBT

TAXES

Taxes are the monies that are needed to carry out what the people decide that the government should do, through their elected representatives, but we have been laboring under an ancient understanding of taxes—that it is what the king takes from people to what he wants to do. We need to change our conception of taxes from this ancient one to a more democratic one. I will press the country to view taxes not as something being taken from citizens but rather as money to pay for what the citizens agree to do together as a country. That is what government is for—to provide a mechanism for doing what the citizens agree to do together, through their elected representatives in Congress, that they can't do individually. (Monies for the Armed Forces and for highways are examples of this.) In this view of taxes, citizens can be proud of contributing their money to carrying out our spending decisions (determined by our elected representatives), rather than trying to find every possible way to avoid contributing by avoiding taxes. People who contribute the most in taxes should be the ones recognized and praised, not those who figure out ways to pay the least!

We give a wrong impression of taxes by expecting the same amount of taxes every year from the tax-paying citizens. This makes it seem like the government is taking something from you for no given reason. We should look at it as something we contribute to make up the amount that Congress has decided that the government will spend. I believe that it would make Congress more responsible if the government got in taxes not a standard portion of our money each year (as it does now, by getting a percentage of our income) but only enough each year to pay for what the elected representatives had decided to spend the previous year. If Congress decides to spend more, then citizens should pay more, and if Congress decides to spend less, then citizens would pay less. There is no need, then, for periodic tax reductions or tax breaks or fighting about tax amounts. Our taxes will be exactly what your Congress wants to spend. If your representatives are spending too much, then you can elect other people.

The disadvantage of this is that you would not know for sure from one year to the next what your taxes were going to be, but again, giving voters more chances to elect representatives with whom they agree about spending is worth the loss of certainty. Congresspersons will want to keep spending fairly uniform from year to year, in order to get fewer complaints from citizens about the variation!

I am interested in the flat-tax idea but don't have enough information about it. One thing I like about the idea is doing away with most deductions, and I think that everyone should participate in paying taxes, regardless of income.

I will provide citizens with more information about what is being spent. You will see how much goes for basic services, how much for healthcare, how much for defense, etc. No attempt has been made to interpret the immense federal budget for citizens, probably because elected officials would rather that citizens not see exactly what is going on.

We also need a revision regarding who pays taxes. Everyone should pay their share of basic service costs (the military, the roads, water, etc.), and this includes the poor and our internet companies. Everyone should have "skin in the game" and should have a share of the responsibility for determining how the country is run. Not having to pay taxes should not be a reward for anyone! The excuse of internet companies not paying taxes because it will reduce "innovation" is no longer applicable. Huge internet companies will do all they can to innovate in order to compete for business, and they do not need a free ride any longer.

The tax code should not be used as a convenient mechanism for rewarding some citizens and harming others. We don't need thousands of pages of deductions. It may be convenient to give certain citizens tax deductions (for installing solar panels, or buying a house, etc.), but this leads to the attitude that it is good to avoid taxes whenever possible. If people are to be rewarded for installing solar panels, they should get a check for that from the government, rather than a tax deduction. If we want to make it easier for people to buy a house (at the expense of renters and others), we should give them a check for that, rather than a tax deduction. This keeps every citizen's responsibility to contribute to government separate from the things that government wants to encourage. We should be encouraging people to pay taxes, not giving them an out. This approach would mean somewhat more administration, but it would make tax computation much simpler and would lead to fewer audits, and it would preserve the purity of taxes as funding for what we as a country decide to do, rather than as a mechanism for taking care of all these other things we want to encourage.

In addition to this "pay as you go" system, there will also be a "rainy day" fund equivalent to one year's spending on average, which will be in a trust that prevents Congress from seeking to spend it except for true emergencies. This approach will make borrowing by the government unnecessary, and Congress will approve each year the amount by which we wish to pay down the national debt (which will then be part of our taxes for that year).

Note that this philosophy of taxes does away with accusations that the government is "socialist," by which accusers mean that the government is taking an inappropriate amount of control of society. If the people, through Congress, approve money for things, then it can't be socialism to do those things (unless the government is taking over the means of production), because those things are what the people (through their properly elected representatives) have decided to do.

Technically, "socialism" means that the government controls the decisions about what products to make and how many of them and may own the factories that produce them, but certain persons wanting to get elected have changed the common meaning of socialism to mean instead that the government provides things for the citizens, which of course could apply just as well to defending the country or providing healthcare for the elderly who cannot afford it, which we do not call socialism.

Other Opinions
The public has no idea what their taxes pay for and are therefore opposed to any tax hike, and you will never convince them to pay more, even for worthy projects. No Congressperson can stay in office if he/she advocates for higher taxes, so the only way to pay for what people want is to borrow more.

A BALANCED BUDGET, BORROWING, AND THE NATIONAL DEBT

We as a country must deal with the real world, and in the real world you have to pay for what you get. There is no place, except in emergencies, for overspending and borrowing to pay for it or for expecting future generations to pay your bills. Government borrowing is the way that Congress has learned to spend more without asking citizens to pay for it. There is tremendous self-interest for Congresspersons to spend money for their constituents, since they hope that will induce voters to re-elect them, but this selfish self-interest makes life worse for all citizens by giving a false sense of what they are paying for with their tax dollars and by adding the interest on the national debt to what taxpayers have to pay. Since borrowing always means that you will pay significantly more than you would have if you had not borrowed, we can maximize the use of our tax dollars by borrowing not at all or as little as necessary. Congress can borrow like this assuming that by the time citizens must pay back the money, they themselves will be retired and won't have to deal with it at all—a very irresponsible attitude! Congressional borrowing has also contributed to the public assuming that borrowing is a "good thing" that can be done with no worries about the future, which has caused many unwary citizens many problems of indebtedness.

I will strive very hard to have a balanced budget every year (even if my plan to have the next year's taxes pay for this year's spending is not adopted). I will work to have Congress identify for every bill the costs for citizens in their next year's taxes (showing what it will cost with borrowing and without borrowing), so you can see what is going on.

Because the nation has come to love immediate consumption based on borrowing, while ignoring that everything paid for through borrowing costs much more than it would cost if it were paid for immediately, without borrowing, action must be taken to ensure budgetary responsibility. I will work to drastically restrict (and eliminate if possible) government borrowing and will establish a rainy day fund available only for declared emergencies. If Congress does not make available estimates of the cost to taxpayers of each bill they pass, then I will estimate the amount of tax dollars needed to pay for the activities proposed in every Congressional bill and every presidential proposal, with borrowing and without, so that citizens may see the costs. (As an example, in considering using taxpayer money for citizens who do not have health insurance (the Affordable Healthcare Act), it would have been more fair initially to calculate what it would cost each taxpayer to pay for that healthcare for others and then ask citizens whether they wanted to pay that much for that purpose, via a referendum to guide Congress about the peoples' position on healthcare for all.)

I will press for a standard policy of committing the money for each activity approved by Congress at the time Congress votes to approve it (either the identification of monies in the current tax income that are available to pay for the activity, or adding it to the following year's tax bill for citizens). Otherwise, I will veto these actions, or these actions will have to wait until some other year. Funds may also be accumulated for activities pursuant to legislation over time, through a "savings" plan approved at the time of the bill, and such funds being saved will be inviolate, so that no one can take monies from any of these funds for other purposes.

I will not support raising the national debt one more dollar but will instead insist as far as I can that we as citizens not spend beyond our means, since the government has no money of its own but only the money that we citizens give it in taxes. Currently we go through the disgraceful charade of Congress passing a spending bill and then haggling later over raising the national debt to pay for it, when they have already approved the spending! I will oppose all efforts to "raise the debt ceiling," since it will be so much better long-term if we learn to live with what we are willing to pay for. If we have to tighten our belts in some regards in some years, this will help us by making clear what we get for our money, instead of having citizens think falsely that the government can afford anything it wants by printing money if it needs to. Congress should include in every year's budget a certain amount for paying down the exorbitant national debt that they have accumulated.

Other Opinions

Since we can't raise taxes, the only way to pay for what voters want is to borrow more. Voters don't have to pay for that right away, and no one can convince them to pay right now for all that they want. When we reach the current debt ceiling, we can try to look good by bargaining our votes for some tiny reductions in spending, but we can't talk to the voters about reducing spending, since that would take away things they want us to pay for without paying more themselves. It's a tough position for us to be in!

MAKING ELECTIONS ABOUT WHO CAN DO THE JOB BEST

CHOOSING A PRESIDENT

Even though the U.S. President has limited power to unilaterally change things in the country, he or she is the symbolic leader of the country and has considerable influence over the future of citizens. Since the job of President is complicated and requires making good decisions about complex matters, as well as kissing babies and reassuring the citizens, it would seem valuable to consider just what skills and traits a President would have to have in order to do the best possible job as President. Unfortunately, there is almost no public discussion of this, even in election years. Voting decisions are made in a number of ways by citizens, including:

- voting for the party's candidate rather than for an individual candidate, even when the party's candidate may not actually represent the beliefs of the party (e.g., Donald Trump, 2016)
- voting for the whole slate of the party
- voting for the candidate that someone else is going to vote for (a parent, a friend, someone one respects), without trying to consider who is best qualified
- voting for the candidate who agrees with one on a single issue that is important to one, such as abortion, unions, the environment, or war
- voting for the candidate who seems most aggressive (and therefore supposedly best for defending the country or waging war)
- voting for the candidate who is best looking
- voting for the candidate who comes from one's own part of the country

- voting for the candidate with the greatest name recognition, even though that recognition may not be entirely positive
- flipping a coin
- voting for the candidate who promises the most (even though these promises by presidential candidates are almost never fulfilled, since the President does not have the power to actually make these thing happen but must have agreement from Congress and/or the courts)
- voting for the candidate who justifies and expands one's grievances
- voting for the candidate who seems most like oneself
- voting for the person whose name appears at the top of the ballot
- voting for the candidate whose campaign has done the most negative advertising (or, alternatively, voting for the candidate whose campaign has done the least amount of negative advertising)
- voting for the candidate that one "likes" best
- voting for the candidate with whom one would most like to share a meal or a beer
- considering a range of issues that are important to the country and matching up those issues with the candidates' positions
- carefully evaluating the personal traits and abilities of candidates to do the job of President well

Only the last two of these consciously aim at electing the best qualified candidate, so it is little wonder that Presidents who are elected vary a great deal in fitness for office! For some voters, the use of intuition, based on various social cues, may help them rule out some unqualified candidates, but careful attention to actual job functions and associated skills would identify the most qualified candidate even better (assuming that voters can know what the abilities of a particular candidate are).

JOB TASKS OF THE PRESIDENT

The President engages in the following activities (if he/she is to be maximally effective):

- after carefully considering various alternatives, identifies what seems to be the best solution to a problem or the best policy to follow (with regard to problems and issues that are usually quite

complex and require research, lengthy reading, and gathering opinions from "experts" and advisors), while still aware that such decisions may need to be updated as more information becomes available
- proposes the above solutions/policies to the public and to Congress, with supportive reasons and data
- organizes support for his/her positions among legislators and the public
- compromises on solutions/policies when doing so is demanded by the exigency of the situation and the impact on the public
- hires and appoints a multitude of government officials and administrative advisers
- considers all citizens and their needs, not just those he/she likes or identifies with, and seeks solutions that are in an overall sense best for the country
- acts as commander-in-chief of the country's armed forces; inspires the troops; makes military decisions with the advice of generals; seeks Congressional approval or support for what he/she views as needed military actions
- determines foreign policy, considering the needs of the U.S., the values of the U.S., and the impacts on other countries, with an emphasis on cooperation and mutual benefit whenever possible
- interacts with leaders of foreign nations and groups in order to build relationships and obtain cooperation
- informs citizens about problems, solutions, and policies
- inspires citizens to be "good citizens" and participate in community and government
- lives by values that inspire citizens (setting an ethical example and modeling adaptive ways of relating to other citizens)
- maintains objectivity by not being motivated to become President for personal aggrandizement, power, or pride but rather to serve the country and its people
- engages in symbolic actions that engender a feeling of togetherness on the part of all citizens (christening submarines, kissing babies, opening shopping centers, hosting Easter egg rolls, inspecting sites of disasters, etc.)

The most qualified President is the one who can do the greatest number of these things well, with legislative, military, and foreign policy functions weighted more heavily.

HOW DO I MATCH UP?

- after carefully considering various alternatives, identifies what seems to be the best solution to a problem or the best policy to follow
  I am a careful decision-maker, gathering facts and opinions before settling on the best solution. I base decisions on extensive data-gathering and am immediately responsive to new information that changes how we should approach things. I have years of experience integrating evolving knowledge about psychological assessment and treatment with changing governmental regulations to produce a training program that has all the needed information for trainees, gives them meaningful experiences applying what they are learning, and keeps all the administrators and lawyers happy. I will identify knowledge-experts in economics, ethics, taxation, management, etc., with whom to consult and will of course use my cabinet members and the Joint Chiefs of Staff extensively.
- proposes the above solutions/policies to the public and to Congress, with supportive reasons and data
  I am good at organizing information and making it understandable. I wrote the charting/medical records manual for our mental health department, and my experience analyzing legislation will make reviewing the work of Congress easier. I frequently had to present changes in my training program to department administrators who were not clinicians, so I know how to phrase things to be both accurate and understandable. I also revised the Constitution and Ethics Code for the Inland Psychological Association and the By-Laws of the Education and Training Division of the California Psychological Association.
- organizes support for his/her positions among legislators and the public
  I am persuasive with information but not so good at soliciting support, since I believe that each person should make his/her own decisions after being given a fair representation of current knowledge. I will never, of course, engage in "dealing" or vote-trading, since I see them as destructive to democracy.
- compromises on solutions/policies when doing so is demanded by the exigency of the situation and the impact on the public
  I am very good at reconciling various opinions by identifying factors that bring benefit to as many stakeholders as possible.

I strongly believe that leaders must advance the country's status in as many areas as possible, whenever possible, which makes compromising necessary. We can never make things perfect but must do as well as we possibly can. I see a good compromise as a win for everyone.

- hires and appoints a multitude of government officials and administrative advisers

  I am good at evaluating people and their strengths and weaknesses and have much experience at doing this. I am not extensively "connected" in academic and financial circles and will need to rely on the contacts of advisers to fill many important positions.

- considers all citizens and their needs, not just those he/she likes or identifies with, and seeks solutions that are in an overall sense best for the country

  I am very good at involving all sides and at considering all of the likely consequences of various courses of action. My sense of fairness requires of me that I consider the impact of decisions on everyone before acting. I organized my training program through a Training Committee consisting of supervisors who each had their own philosophies of care, and I brought them all together to agree on the basic structure of our program.

- acts as commander-in-chief of the country's armed forces; inspires the troops; makes military decisions with the advice of generals; seeks Congressional approval or support for what he/she views as needed military actions

  My seven years in the Air Force gives me a fair understanding about how the military works, and I am completely prepared to make difficult decisions in this area (with appropriate advice from the Joint Chiefs, of course). I think that the U.S. has gotten overly involved in country-building using the military in the past and will avoid that myself. I strongly believe that Congress must be involved at every step of the way whenever U.S. troops are at risk around the world. For my trainee group, I had to keep their spirits up and keep them inspired about their clinical work even when administrators put obstacles in our path.

- determines foreign policy, considering the needs of the U.S., the values of the U.S., and the impacts on other countries, with an emphasis on cooperation and mutual benefit whenever possible

  Other countries' rights and needs are just as important to the future of our country as our own rights and needs in this increasingly interdependent world, and other countries will react positively to being treated fairly and with concern. I believe that our sense of ethics should apply to all people all around the globe, and not just to our own society.

- interacts with leaders of foreign nations and groups in order to build relationships and obtain cooperation

  I am a good team player and do not need to assert primacy in relationships with other countries, while at the same time not allowing ourselves to be taken advantage of in any way. I am good at finding win-win solutions to problems. I will be pressing Congress to ratify treaties and other agreements that they have in the past been unwilling to do.

  I formed an association of training programs in the Los Angeles area to share information and updates about training. This involved bringing together equals and helping them to work together.

- informs citizens about problems, solutions, and policies

  I am very good at explaining all the pros and cons of issues and believe that citizens should be given both (all) sides of issues instead of only what I think is best. I will give weekly televised or internet presentations informing citizens about current issues and concerns. In my Training Committee meetings, I presented options for meeting our requirements, and together we sorted out what was most acceptable.

- inspires citizens to be "good citizens" and participate in community and government

  I believe that greater involvement of citizens in community affairs and in advising government are both crucial to bringing us together to do the best work possible for our country. I will welcome more citizen feedback and will organize regular referenda on big issues. As noted above, I had to support and inspire my trainees even when the going was tough.

- lives by values that inspire citizens (setting an ethical example and modeling adaptive ways of relating to other citizens)

  I will live my values with consistency and integrity at all times (as explained in this document). As a leader I will at all times act as a caring and responsible adult. You can check this out by contacting those I have worked with over the years.

- maintains objectivity by not being motivated to become President for personal aggrandizement, power, or pride but rather to serve the country and its people

I want to serve as President not for personal gain or fame but to be a healing factor in our present circumstances. I enjoy helping people solve problems and be happy! I am very good at thinking independently no matter what people around me are saying and very good at not being influenced by lobbying and salesmanship.
- engages in symbolic actions that engender a feeling of togetherness on the part of all citizens (christening submarines, kissing babies, opening shopping centers, hosting Easter egg rolls, inspecting sites of disasters, etc.)

I prefer spending time working on issues and problems rather than seeking PR opportunities, but I understand that the President must do a certain amount of inspiring and public posturing. I like people, though, and will have no trouble with being with them and celebrating our shared love of the country and our fellow citizens.

Voters are cautioned against choosing a candidate to vote for on the basis of only a few criteria. The President's job is multi-faceted, and a candidate with whom you disagree on the issue most important to you may do you more good on ten other issues, so it may be in your best interest to vote for that candidate in this election.

See Appendix A for a rating scale to be used to compare candidates for the presidency.

Other Opinions

We can't educate voters to know much about candidates, so we have to compete with slogans and emotional manipulation. Otherwise they won't vote at all. You have way too much faith in what citizens will do to have a well-functioning democracy!

JOBS FOR ALL AND WAGES FOR A DECENT LIFE

JOBS FOR ALL

As a psychologist, I am convinced that people feel better when they are doing something effective in the world that in their opinions contributes to their own welfare and also to the general welfare of their groups (family, nation, etc.). The relevance of their actions to their welfare was more straightforward in past eras for hunter-gatherers who got up every day and went out to find food. Nowadays, we do it by "working" at a "job," which narrows our vision of our contributions so that it is less clear to us that we are doing something important for the group. The fact is that every worker is contributing to something important—the greater welfare of the nation. Our systems for making food and shelter available for all of us would not work without the work done by each of the individuals in those industries, and those individuals should be proud of what they are contributing. Similarly, those working in government at each level should be proud, and the purpose of their work and contributions should be more even more clear. Of course, there are always some workers who sluff off and don't contribute much, but if the importance for other citizens of their work was more clear to them, perhaps they would feel better about themselves and their jobs. Working in other industries, such as entertainment, provides something worthwhile for citizens, too, even though it is not as essential.

It is also true that many without jobs, including those whom we deem to be disabled, could perform useful services, even though they cannot compete with able-bodied workers in a capitalist hiring system (where businesses try to hire only the most qualified and the least costly). Dealing with part-time workers is more trouble for businesses than having only full-time workers, but it is very possible for businesses to make good use of part-time workers, and it would be better for those workers to have a job and be doing something useful than to be out of the workforce, as well as being better for the country to have them working and contributing.

We have thought that businesses had no responsibility for job creation for the nation and should do it only to make more money, assuming that individuals could always find a job for themselves. This is changing due to a more complex economy, greater need for workers with specialized experience, off-shoring of jobs, and moving factories and headquarters around. A large part of the white supremacy protests about immigration have been by young men out of work who are blaming it on immigrants, but this is a tiny part of the explanation. American businesses have been "all about" the bottom line and very little about playing a part in a national economy, which includes not just making money but also providing work for part of the nation's workforce.

It's good to have a low unemployment rate like our current four percent, and we tend to accept this as "good enough" without noting that four percent of the population is approximately twelve million people who are seeking jobs but cannot find them. These twelve million need jobs, for their sake and for the sake of having a stable and happy country. As noted above, globalization has put a significant number of citizens out of work, and those displaced need to work, regardless of whether businesses at their most efficient can produce those jobs. It is more important for the nation for everyone to be working and contributing than it is for businesses to be functioning at their most efficient.

The nation as a whole must take care of all of its citizens, and a crucial element in people feeling good about themselves and their nation is working and contributing. Businesses are therefore not just set up to make money for a select few, but they also have a responsibility to participate in providing opportunities for people to work (and of course they should benefit from doing so, as well).

The increasing specialization of jobs has meant that finding another job when laid off is more difficult now than it used to be, and the reluctance of many people to move to where they could find another job (and leave their familiar surroundings) also contributes to people not finding work.

In order to enable every person who can work to work and contribute, I will move to set up job-finding assistance for all citizens, either federally or through the states (using already established job development agencies in each state), and I will seek funding to guarantee a job for everyone, even if it has to be a temporary one and even if it is street sweeping, ditch digging, or janitorial, created by some level of government (envelope stuffers?, park workers?, trash collectors?, extra clerical help?, extra warehouse help?). This will allow many people now unable to find jobs to work and to feel like they are contributing to society. These earnings could replace "welfare" in some (perhaps all) cases. "Unemployment" programs for workers will probably continue (for the interims between jobs), but *there will be no other government assistance for those who refuse these temporary jobs (unless they are truly unable to work)* (no food stamps, no childcare, etc.).

The job-development agency could approach businesses or government offices to offer workers/positions that would be completely government supported (at perhaps the level of fast-food workers, if the decent-life proposal below is not implemented). Businesses could also approach the job-development agency to arrange for these positions.

The nation as a whole bears the responsibility to provide work opportunities for everyone. When working was a matter simply of walking out the door into the forest or to the ocean and finding food, we could leave it completely to individuals to get out there and find food, but in this day and age, such opportunities are not available to most of us, so the nation as a whole must set up systems for making it happen—for matching people to jobs. *Businesses and taxpayers, then, should both be paying part of the salary cost for these jobs* (even for "make work" jobs, if you want to consider them that). Citizens with these jobs will then be spending most of their salaries in the economy. The benefit of the work (and the resulting spending) to the general economy is worth more than this taxpayer money, and hopefully many of these jobs will become permanent as workers prove their worth.

This job-finding aid, together with job retraining, will also be increasingly important for more and more people as our economy moves toward the use of more robots and becomes more and more a service economy (which puts manual laborers and factory workers at a severe disadvantage). We can no longer leave job finding and retraining completely to the workers themselves, as we have always done in the past, since it was not their choice to globalize our economy and not their choice to move to robotics, which has led to the obsolescence of many jobs once considered to be good jobs for supporting a family. The fact that employers increasingly only want to hire people with experience in the job makes changing employment areas very difficult for workers who are let go, so *former employers and the government must pay for new training*. This job service will have a cost to taxpayers, but the emotional benefit and the productivity benefit of having more people working seem to me to outweigh the cost.

Many will object to this job-finding aid and to providing jobs for those who cannot find them, claiming that if people don't have to struggle and try hard, they will sink into apathy and be poor workers, but if we make contributing to the common good a value, then every useful job will justify some pride and respect for the worker. Also, as stated above, there will be no government aid for those refusing to work. This will bring up problems in evaluating who is able to work and who is genuinely not able to work, but these problems are less important than getting everybody involved in working.

Bear in mind, too, that as we utilize artificial intelligence and robots more and more, we will be creating a growing class of people out of work and with no prospect of work, so we will either need to create jobs on purpose for those left out or pay them not to work. I suspect that paying people not to work will be more noxious to conservatives than making jobs for them! Some will claim that every job revolution (industrialization, microelectronics) creates even more jobs, but while this has happened in the past, it is not guaranteed. I believe that we will reach a dead end in "progress," due to losing cheap energy, rising population, and climate change and will have to share more and work together more in order to survive, instead of leaving everyone to fend for himself or herself.

Some will claim pessimistically that people won't work unless they are forced to, but I believe that every citizen would like to feel proud of contributing to the overall good of the nation (not just in wartime), so it will pay us to develop a new attitude about work—that it is not just about getting a paycheck but also about contributing to the common good.

There will have to be serious discussions about exemptions from the work requirement. For instance, will wanting to stay in one's home town be an acceptable justification for not working (and still receiving government money to supplement other income). There are arguments to be made in both directions!

Other Opinions

Helping people find jobs and in effect forcing them to work (!) are extreme government intrusion into what we expect citizens to do for themselves (and they are by and large doing it pretty well). It will be better to leave things the way they are, and perhaps increase the "safety net" to take better care of those who aren't working.

People need to have "skin in the game," including finding their own jobs. Otherwise they will just be lazy workers who miss a lot of days when they should be working. Human beings don't work unless they have to.

Finding jobs for people is just another move toward socialism and a nanny-state.

WAGES FOR A DECENT LIFE

Our relatively "raw capitalism" approach to employment puts all the responsibility for finding jobs on workers, and this, plus employers' desires not to pay benefits, have resulted in many jobs in our economy that don't pay enough to enable their workers to survive and have a decent life. It is unacceptable for the richest nation in the world to have a significant percentage of citizens (perhaps twenty percent?) unable to have a decent life due to lack of income. (See "Jobs For All" for a proposal for significant job-finding assistance for workers.) Most entry-level jobs now require that the worker live with parents or someone else and go without health insurance (at least for young singles) rather than being able to be truly self-supporting. *I will advocate for making all full-time jobs provide income at a level at which one could survive and have a decent life (with part-time jobs pro-rated).* Part of this would be provided by employers and part by government, through our taxes.

A "decent life" must be defined, of course, and a government commission and ultimately Congress will have to decide what a decent life is (what size house, what size TV, what health insurance, etc.) Under this plan, every full-time worker would receive at least the "decent life" amount for the year. (Persons in part-time jobs would receive this level of pay pro-rated.) This would change nothing for those workers already at or above this decent-life income level. Employers would continue to compete for higher-wage and more specialized workers just as they do now.

Some employers have scrimped on wages by paying only part-time and giving workers different schedules every week (which keep them from taking second jobs). These practices will be discouraged. Jobs should be consolidated into full-time as much as possible.

One way to finance this effort would be to make it totally employer-supported, through setting the minimum wage at the decent-life level (perhaps $18 per hour, for a gross income of $35,000 for a single person), but this would certainly be unpopular with employers. This method would have the least administrative cost. However, it can be argued that all citizens should have a role in supporting our least well-paid citizens, because the rest of us care about the welfare of those least well-paid citizens (and are appropriately grateful for the fact that we don't need this support ourselves).

This program is more likely to be instituted if the government pays a supplement to the employers' contributions (wages) at some business-tolerable level ($15 per hour?), and we make up through taxes the difference between what was paid by the employer and what is needed for a decent life. This wage for a decent life, if paid for completely by employers would increase consumer prices (for fast food, restaurant meals, and any goods and services produced by workers who are not now paid a living wage).

People will be required to work at whatever level of skill and hours per week that they are able, and if they choose not to work, they will not be eligible for any government assistance including the "decent life" money. I believe that doing work that makes a worker feel good about utilizing his/her abilities and feel good about contributing to society will be satisfying and fulfilling, but our species has evolved to take the easiest way to a goal, and there will be some who would like to go this route (take free money) rather than work.

Some will claim that that if people don't have enough money for a decent life, they must not be working hard enough, but it is a fact that the army of fast food workers and many others (including the "gig economy") do not make enough working full-time to support themselves.

It is claimed that employers would "have to" lay off workers and raise prices if they were forced to increase pay, but we should find out in real life whether consumers will pay the new prices (and adjust elsewhere in their budgets) or do without those goods and services. If it is the case that citizens would pay for goods and services at the higher prices, then perhaps tax revenue would not be needed to fund the decent-life effort.

Depending on public support and on the true costs (that can only be known by trying it out), adjustments would certainly be made to this initiative. If anyone has a better idea for how all Americans who work can receive enough for a decent life, it will certainly be considered! If business doesn't like paying higher wages, then business can formulate another way to accomplish what is in effect a redistribution.

The devil is always in the details, of course, so it is important that this initiative be well planned. I believe that around 20 percent of workers will need this supplement to reach the "decent life" level.

(1) The level of income needed for a "decent life" will be set regionally and recomputed every year. I personally do not have the resources to make a really good estimate of this level or of the overall costs of such a program as this, but the levels might be $35,000 for single persons and $45,000 for families.

(2) All new positions added by businesses would be eligible for government assistance if this program goes into effect. The job-finding agency (such as state employment development agencies that would be used for the job-finding described in "Jobs For All") would estimate the portion of the wage for the new position that the business should contribute. (This has implications for government wage-setting in general, but not for government price-setting. This issue will certainly require more discussions.)

(3) If there is a government-supplied supplement to wages, the employer will not be allowed to lower his/her wages for those jobs (to make government pay it all). This continuing wage level will be adjusted for inflation. The employer could eliminate those jobs, but we would presume that workers would be happier (with the decent life) and would therefore work harder, which would make them more desirable as workers for the employer. In any case, the financial arrangements must be advantageous for the employer, to maintain stable jobs.

(4) Workers receiving the government wage supplement would pay some taxes on their income. Every citizen will contribute something to the nation by way of taxes and will therefore feel more responsible to pay attention to how the government is spending money. There will no longer be a substantial percentage of citizens who pay no income taxes (now around 40 percent?), due to deductions and progressive tax levels.

(5) It is not clear whether a healthcare program such as the Affordable Care Act would automatically provide healthcare for all receiving the wage supplement or become one for which the worker would pay full cost (along with other choices such as private or employer-supported insurance). Perhaps part-time workers would automatically be covered by the government program. The issue would be whether workers should be full consumers in terms of making their own decisions about how to spend their incomes, which is both an economic and a cultural issue.

(6) All citizens (both receiving and not receiving the supplement) will contribute to the money needed for this "decent life" program, through their taxes, but taxes for the very rich (having more than one million dollars of income per year) will be increased (which needs to be done anyway, whether or not there is a wage supplement program).

Another way of approaching this issue would be to generate a pool of money through taxes and then to send everyone a check each month for the same amount. Think of everyone contributing to this pool of money at the same rate (like part of a ten percent flat tax) and everyone then receiving from the pool the same dollar amount of benefit (e.g., $1000 a month). This would be an inconsequential contribution and benefit for those who have more and would be a significant help to those who have less, who could then use that extra money to move to get a better job, for instance or stave off homelessness due to a financial or work catastrophe.

Other Opinions

This proposal would just make us all soft and lazy. It sounds nice and cushy, but it would do damage to our hard-work and self-responsibility ethic, along with driving some businesses out of business.

This is socialism or maybe even communism! Lots of people will try to game the system by pretending they can't work, and citizens are too softhearted to let them starve, so we will always have ten percent of the population that won't participate in the economy, except to sponge off of it. Just accept this as the way things have to be. Don't get into fooling with the market forces that determine our prices.

WELFARE

There has been far too much upset and misinformation over welfare in this country. *I will support both helping people to become contributing citizens and ensuring that people who are not willing to contribute receive no government help, by ensuring that we have productive jobs for every individual and ensuring that those roles result in enough income to have a "decent life." This will include sufficient childcare funding to enable mothers of young children to work (since their jobs are so frequently minimum wage which is insufficient for childcare) and aggressive job-finding by government so that everyone willing to work has the opportunity.* If private business is unable to "create" enough jobs to enable everyone to work, then government will create those jobs. Declining to work when jobs are available will result in aid being cut off. The "decent life" wage idea (see that section of this platform) could eliminate a great deal of what we now call welfare.

Other Opinions

Finally, something we agree on. Welfare should be eliminated, but this does not mean that we should find jobs for everyone. They should have been earning their keep all this time anyway.

HAVING CIVIL DISCOURSE ON SENSITIVE TOPICS

We are all aware of the many voices responding with anger to the very salient political divide in this country currently, and many of us would like both to lessen this divide and to learn to talk with our fellow citizens in reasonable and useful ways about our differences. We all have somewhat different preferences for how we would like things to organized in our country, but to have the cooperation and specialization of functions that enable us to have a complex and wealthy society, we must come to numerous agreements with others, whether that is with a neighbor or with all the citizens of our society (which we do through Congress). We do this using agreed upon behavioral expectations and social forms (talking things over around the kitchen table, talking things over a beer, city council meetings, sessions of Congress).

Currently people seeking elective office emphasize how they will fight for us, as if fighting is necessary just to survive the evil machinations of other citizens. A voter who is unfamiliar with the actual daily workings of Congressional committees and the re-writing of bills might assume (wrongly) that if he doesn't vote for the best fighter, he will lose out. We are much more likely to vote for a "fighter" than for a candidate who promises to "assert our needs and rights" (or heaven forbid, to "be fair to all concerned"), but ask yourself if having some groups of citizens try, for their own benefit, to deny the needs and equality of other citizens is really the kind of country you want.

This fear would not exist unless we doubted the cooperation and good will of other voters across society, and candidates' promises to fight for us cement those doubts. We should know rationally that our governments at every level cannot function without trying to make their solutions to problems palatable to the greatest number of people possible, and we know that in our own families, if there is no compromise or working together to find the most desirable solutions to problems, then some members will be perpetually unhappy. Yet we continue to populate Congress with fighters (rather than solvers) who are very likely to continue to fight until one side "wins" (only temporarily) and the other half of the population is angry and unhappy. The rancor and fighting that we see in the logjam of our governments is the result of wanting to have our way to the exclusion of the needs and feelings of others, and the only way this will change is if we voters insist on some different attitudes in our legislators and other leaders. This, of course, may take some attitude changes in ourselves!

The long-term solution to this sorry state of affairs is to apply the principles of equality, positive attitude, empathy, learning the truth as far as possible, and cooperation that I promote in my campaign. Over the long term, we will all benefit the most by—

- accepting that all citizens' views deserve equal weight in decision-making (even if that means we don't always get our own way),
- viewing others as co-authors with us of our future together (at least until they prove to be enemies),
- trying to learn and understand the views of groups that are different from ourselves, knowing that deep down they have the same emotions and life goals that we do,
- insisting that our elected officials take into account as many voters' views and desires as possible and view all voters as having an equal say in things, and
- voting out of office all legislators who desire to shape the country the way only one group wants it to be.

DISCUSSING POLITICS WISELY AND COMPASSIONATELY

It is taken as a truism that people should avoid discussing politics and religion if they wish to have a civil conversation, but a democracy needs its citizens to share ideas so that the best solutions to problems can arise. It is very possible to have productive and civil conversations about difficult topics if you follow the admonitions and principles above. These principles can be applied, of course, in any relationship, including couples, families, and groups, that need better understanding and cooperation among their members.

(1) The first requirement is to accept that those who differ from your political beliefs are fully human. As advocated here, everyone is fundamen-

tally equal, and we all have the same fundamental goals in life. Therefore, we must open our minds to the views of others if we are to understand them and if we are to care about having them understand us.

(2) As explained by Jonathan Haidt in his book *The Righteous Mind: Why Good People Are Divided By Politics and Religion*, liberals in our society tend to value change (progress) and autonomy (so they frequently want to change things "for the better") while conservatives tend to value tradition, order, hierarchy, and sacredness (and so need good reasons to change and give up the good in what we have already). These are all human value possibilities and by themselves are not evil or destructive. The second requirement for having useful and civil discussions, then, is to accept that the other person's values are worth taking seriously. Liberals should be honest enough to admit that traditions can be useful for societal bonding and order and that pondering the sacred can add depth and empathy to life. Conservatives should be honest enough to admit that our society needs some changes if it is to live up to its ideals of equality and freedom. If you are liberal and want to understand others, admit that change is not always good, and tradition is often useful. If you are conservative, admit that change is sometimes good and that too much adherence to tradition can stymie all improvement. Both liberals and conservatives should formulate to themselves how their political philosophy advances the other side's values and not just their own!

(3) It is also crucial for everyone to accept that his or her "side" is never going to "win" or vanquish the other, particularly since each "side" expresses values that are important for a society to be able to function and endure. We must be willing to live with the best compromises that we can come up with. Deciding on policies that "give" something to both sides is our only way forward. Getting your own way is actually damaging to democracy, since democracy is based on the notion that putting together many different views is the best way to find the best solution possible at the moment, and doing this is unlikely to come out just the way you want! (You might prefer having a king, for example, rather than a democracy, so that there would be only one view at the top, but that means that what you want is a monarchy and not a democracy.)

Difficult discussions must have the goal of creating and maintaining "good," "positive" interactions—interactions in which both parties feel comfortable and safe (as a result of understanding each other and feeling treated appropriately by the other person) and in which the interaction enhances the welfare of both parties. These interactions succeed through understanding and cooperation and result in minimum amounts of conflict and violence between people. We can move toward this goal if we make a habit of thinking of every policy decision as an opportunity to make it a "win-win," for every major side. We can be civil and humane if we (1) focus on understanding why the other person has the views and feelings that he has and (2) learn to make and value effective compromises.

(4) We must not be afraid of the other person or group. Our "news" shows us only the bad side of people (perhaps with one minute at the end of the broadcast for an "inspirational" story), and all news outlets are to some degree biased (even CNN and NPR). Human beings construct their worlds out of what they observe and experience, so if they see only violence, they conclude that the whole world is violent. Face-to-face exposure to members of groups we fear can be a great help. The more we see the humanity of others and can identify with others, the less fear we have of them.

(5) One must not believe that the other person or group is evil. This may be difficult if your religious group promotes the concept of evil and uses fear of evil as a means of assisting members to maintain self-control. It also makes caring for people who are different from you difficult.

(6) No one has the right to claim that his or her values should dominate society. We cannot eliminate those who think differently; we must live with them, as equals and not as captives or de facto slaves. Try to view differences as things to explore and learn about. There is no objective reason to say that any one value stance is automatically any better or more true than another (although we can compare the results of attempts to live by various value sets).

(7) Too often discussions about differences are approached by both parties with the aim of changing the other person's mind so that they will be more like us. This is practically a guarantee of failure in the discussion, since both parties will be defensive and/or aggressive in manner, which makes better understanding impossible. Give up the idea that you can get others to see things exactly as you do. The main reason they don't is not because they are stupid or stubborn but because they have had different lives than yours. The growing urban—rural split in our society illustrates the negative result of people living apart and having no idea how the other half lives.

The way to accept that you can't get everyone to agree with you and still get value from political discussions is to change your focus from trying to convince the other person to agree with you to trying to understand his unique viewpoint. Understanding both your viewpoint and his viewpoint will allow you to see useful potential compromises more easily.

(8) Our American emphasis on winning tends to push us to fight those with whom we differ (war on drugs, war on poverty, winner-take-all elections), as if one side will win and the other lose. Persons who are going to understand and basically accept each other must accept that all positive values and viewpoints can be useful.

If we could treat everyone with respect and courtesy and avoid disapproving of them for our discussions, this could be enough for us to have useful and civil discussions, but few people are prepared emotionally to do this without accepting the above principles and adjusting their negative instinctual reactions to things that they find disagreeable. We must stop trying to win and work toward finding the compromises that are good or at least acceptable for all.

(9) If we agree to take the views of others seriously with the hope of eventually finding the best compromises possible, then the purpose of sharing ideas about public policy must be to understand why the others' views "make sense" given his life experience, rather than trying to change his views to be like ours.

(10) It helps to make your discussions civil to have the assumption that all persons have basic value just for being human.

(11) In our discussions we must treat all others at all times with basic respect and courtesy. Some people feel that if they treat an opponent with respect that this means that they are "giving in" or agreeing with the opponent, but this is not so. You can treat a person with whom you disagree with respect and courtesy and still completely disagree.

(12) The purpose of political discourse cannot be to take advantage of others, since this just makes things worse, so stop trying to take advantage of others, and accept that you cannot get more as a citizen than you are willing to allow others to have.

(13) It will help the relationships between discussants if you acknowledge when the other person has made a potentially useful point. This doesn't mean that you agree with everything the other person says, nor does it mean that you are changing your position.

(14) It will help you to keep your feelings under control if you assume that others are doing the best they can (just as you are doing the best you can), even when they disagree with you. If you make an effort to understand others, you will see that we are all motivated and trying every day to reach our goals, which are basically the same for all human beings—to survive, have no more than tolerable pain, have some times of positive

feelings (mainly through feeling secure and feeling positively about ourselves), have sex and raise children, have some satisfying human relationships, and be accepted in most of our groups (family, town, nation).

(15) In your discussions, stay aware of the needs and situations of *all* citizens, not just those you choose to have contact with. As preparation for discussions, watch and read varied news and political outlets (Wall Street Journal, Fox News, N.Y. Times, Fox cable news, CNN, etc.). Go to community functions where you can interact with those who have different views than yours. Otherwise, you will lose touch with many of the country's citizens. You may anticipate that such contact will be unpleasant, but you will find that if you see others as human beings trying to reach the same basic goals, it will ease your mind.

(16) Go into the interaction with a positive attitude, thinking that you will learn something interesting! Do not set it up in your mind as a battle or a challenge. Nothing someone else could say could invalidate your point of view, and nothing you could say will invalidate the other person's point of view. Your points of view are different because you have different life experiences.

(17) If you can come to the discussion with the above values in mind, then the first thing to actually do when you sit down together is to spend sufficient time finding out about the other person, rather than trying to put forth your own positions. Ask questions rather than make statements. Ask about his background and what it was like for him growing up. Ask about what he wanted to be when he grew up and how that changed over time. Ask about his job and how he sees himself being treated by the overall economic system. Ask about how he would like the country to be in the future and what would help it to get there. Ask about how he views other citizens and how he feels about them. Ask about his experience with those who are different from him. Don't respond, criticize, or comment about his answers. Your job is to understand, not to evaluate or oppose. (Voting is where you get your chance to oppose.)

Figure out why what he believes is natural (to him) given his background and life experience. How we perceive and feel about how we have been treated, by our parents, our teachers, our employers, our elected officials, and our extended family, are primary forces in making the world seem as it does to us (which is not how the world "really" is, but is why we all have different views of the world). There is no such thing as "I just know it." There are always reasons why you believe what you believe.

(18) Share the same kinds of things about yourself that will make your beliefs "make sense" to the other person in terms of your background

and life experience. Accept the fact that with different background and life experiences, your beliefs *would* be different—no less true (to you), but different. This tells us that no beliefs about political matters are sacred—they are simply someone's belief about what works best, given that person's background and life experience. This getting acquainted process takes time, and both parties must be willing to invest the needed time. That commitment itself signals an interest in the other party that is rare these days.

(19) If the other person is challenging or critical when you share your background or views, you need not walk away. If you don't feel threatened (if you are not ashamed or guilty about who you are and how you got there), there is no need to feel shamed or give up. Stick with information, not justification, and certainly do not counterattack. Understand the other person's challenges or criticisms for what they are—a person's fears about how she will be treated by others (including you).

You must want to explore and understand more than you want the other person to change. Hopefully, since you each have only your own opinion and not the truth, both of you will walk away a little bit changed.

(20) In your assertions, stick to "I" statements and questions ("I believe that ____ would solve this problem best, because I have observed ____ and seen ____ in my life). Avoid "you" statements and telling the other person what she believes and why it is wrong. Don't do what politicians do, which is assert something as a fact that is really an opinion ("The fact is....," "Everyone knows that....," "The truth is....").

(21) When you share your views with the other person, treat it as just information and don't try to make it a justification of your beliefs. Stick to the personal (what you believe and why) rather than arguing political theory (conservative, liberal, libertarian, etc.) unless both participants are knowledgeable enough and objective enough to do that.

(22) If the atmosphere heats up, take a break. Calm self-acceptance (being OK with yourself, not boasting or justifying) will calm the other person and promote an atmosphere of exploration rather than fighting.

(23) Only *after* equal sharing, you may explore how the other person's life information relates to her political opinions – e.g., "How do you think your problem finding good jobs relates to who won the election?" Above all, do not be defensive about yourself or critical of the other person. Your own views make so much sense to you that it is tempting to jump ahead to "How could you possibly believe that?" kinds of questions, but this is tempting only when you can't imagine how anyone could possibly believe

those things. The fact that the other person *does* believe those things *proves* that others can have those views, so your job is to understand why the other person believes those things. Expressions of understanding can aid in this process, such as "I see how what you've experienced in life would lead you to see politicians in the way you do."

(24) Put forth your views on policy questions calmly and illustrate what you believe would be the consequences for society if they were implemented. Question if your own choices in these matters would really benefit everyone or just your own group of people. You are responsible for the impact of your ideas on *everyone* if implemented.

(25) Speaking more loudly or forcefully does not give your views any more weight, nor does calling others names or saying negative things about them. That simply says that you don't know how to make your communication effective.

(26) Beware of exaggerated language in political discourse ("oppression" is in most cases actually harm, and "greed" in many cases is actually desire). If you use these inflammatory words, you will lose the respect of the other person. Politicians and cable news exaggerate all the time, thinking that it it's the best way to keep your attention, but it's just an insult to your intelligence.

(27) In assessing a position, the key questions are (1) whether it is consistent with reality or based on false or shaky beliefs, and (2) what all of its consequences would be if that view determined our law and/or governmental actions. Every policy/law has some negative consequences for someone. If your view is adopted, then you are responsible not only for the results that you like but also for the damage that your policy/law does to some other citizens. Making it easier to declare bankruptcy will be a benefit for some but will cost money for the people they owe.

Make it an expectation that all speeches and writing advocating for any position on an issue (in Congress, in the media, etc.) must include some discussion of both the pros and the cons of that position. Do this in your own discussions and writing. State your position and then point out where or for whom your position doesn't work. State the other person's position fairly, and then point out what it would accomplish as well why you don't think it's the best solution. Do this when you think about and formulate your views. To do this, you will have to admit that you could be at least a little bit wrong! Our habit in this society is to make everything a debate, which encourages people to state only what they want you to believe. We learn much more when both sides must explain the things that are problematic in their positions.

(For more on these issues and values, see my essays "The Solution To All Human Interactional Problems" and "Bridging Societal Differences" on www.livewiselydeeply.com under Societal Problems and under Government.)

Other Opinions

No one is going to take the time to learn why others have the opinions they do or to have the self-discipline to listen! This is like pissing in the wind!

IMMIGRATION

The relatively chaotic situation at our Texas/Mexico border is a shameful disgrace for our country. *I will support enforcing our immigration laws (and getting adequate resources to do it from Congress) when these laws are revised and clarified by Congress. I do not support an "open borders" policy that says that anyone who wants to should be able to reside here, regardless of their past, their impact on the nation, or their appropriateness for contributing to the nation. A nation will not be a nation if it has no control over who is a citizen, and a nation will be unnecessarily disorderly if a significant percentage of residents (perhaps fifteen percent?) are not citizens.* We do wish to benefit as many persons as we can who for safety reasons need to be here, but the notion of the U.S. inviting "teeming masses" to come here is behind us. We do need additional workers, but we do not need hordes of additional workers. The sentimental assumption that every needy person should be able to come here cannot be supported any longer.

Our current situation is the result of years of Congressional failure to update our nation's immigration policy, which removes motivation from any administration to adequately staff our border service. We need to pin down (through legislation) how many immigrants and what kinds of immigrants we want, and then that should be enforced—no exceptions.

An important psychological issue is involved here, too. We are all instinctively somewhat fearful of people who are different from us if we cannot understand them and cannot therefore predict with comfort their next behaviors. We can learn to live comfortably with people we "understand," even if they are different, if we decide to, but being around people who are "different" takes a certain amount of extra energy from us. Having large groups of people in a society who are "different" from each other also makes for political conflict and poses some threat to the society's sense of unity. For these reasons, it is best for the total number of immigrants at any one time (persons who have been in the country five years of less, let's say) to be below some percentage of our total population, which allows for immigration but also maintains that sense of national unity. My estimate is that that percentage is around 15 percent. (Think about how it might feel to you to have one in five of the people around you be significantly different from you, which is what it would be like if, for example, that percentage were 20 percent.) This figure determines a base total amount of yearly admissions which can then be divided up among the various categories of immigrants that Congress sees as desirable.

Currently, the largest number of people seeking to enter our country as immigrants are seeking entry under asylum status. The current definition of asylum (reasonable fear of being harmed by one's home government because of one's membership in a defined racial or political group) could be used, if we were willing to enforce it, but the concept of "asylum" in common parlance has been stretched out of recognizable shape to include fear of harm from any source (such as gangs) and for any reason, such as fear of not being able to support one's familyl. The asylum concept must be redefined by Congress, even if this is different from the definition in the treaty which gives us the current definition.

Congress has the power to define who shall be admitted as immigrants. It can admit certain numbers of persons from specific other countries (such as Venezuela), and certain numbers of persons in categories of persons of whom we need more, such as nuclear scientists, microbiologists, physicists, electronic chip and server experts, doctors, etc. Congress should decide every five years what those quotas should be.

Currently persons legally in the U.S. can work toward bringing in other family members regardless of their qualifications under current immigration law ("chain immigration"). This seems currently somewhat reckless, and perhaps should be limited to two or three additional family members. (This would help to control the total number of immigrants.)

The hearing process needs change as well. The applicant's word alone about dangers faced in the home country cannot be simply assumed to be true if we are to have a fair system, and few applicants present documentation to justify their fears. This then requires at present a sort of trial in which the purpose is to tell whether the applicant is telling the truth. Of course, if the applicant has evidence of his/her membership in a protected group (under asylum) and there is public knowledge (newspapers, State Dep't.) of the persecution of that group by that nation's government, then we could grant asylum with good conscience, but without that evidence, asylum should not be granted and the person should be deported, harsh as that may sound. We must protect our process from lying. Perhaps we could spread the word not to come here for asylum if one has no written evidence of danger. Requiring application for asylum status while still at home or in another country may also be useful.

In addition to asylum status, another major reason for having immigrants is that as a country our fertility rate is not high enough to keep up with predicted future job needs, so we need a certain number of immigrants to supply us with additional workers. Guest worker programs should be established and must be adequate to provide the transient labor that some of our businesses require to survive.

After we have a revised immigration policy, then we have a responsibility as a country to enforce the law and to allot enough money (or get it through additional taxes) to properly process the large flow of persons wishing to reside here. At the moment this would include multiplying the number of detention, processing, and hearing facilities at our southwest border. The burden of immigrant flows should not fall on or be borne by border communities. I will press Congress to get to work on a revised and comprehensive immigration policy.

There are other issues regarding non-citizens in our country, such as the significant number who enter the country as visitors and stay illegally. *Non-citizens, (tourists, visitors and immigrants) who are in this country should be tracked and must leave the country when their visas expire. Personnel must be assigned to monitor all aliens in the country. Persons who are in the country illegally must be deported whenever discovered (most likely starting after an amnesty of some sort is offered).* Visas for visits should continue to be easily obtained (with appropriate scrutiny for those who could have terrorist intentions).

I think we should assume that immigrants who want to stay in this country want to become citizens (otherwise they are profiting from the system without contributing enough to it), and it should be required that all immigrants seek citizenship. It is not wise to continually increase the number of residents who are not citizens and therefore not full participants in our overall culture. Again, a nation with a large portion of its residents who are not citizens cannot continue to be unified. The citizenship process should be made much more timely and welcoming through a friendly and supportive immigration and naturalization service.

Some will think me to be not compassionate with regard to immigrants, but it is important to help as many persons in need as we can within the framework of our laws. It damages our legal system to have laws that everyone ignores or manipulates, as we are doing now. It harms the rest of the citizens of our country and harms the country itself to admit immigrants illegally or by ignoring the law. The compassionate route is to assess and empathize with the needs of all (citizens, too, and not just immigrants) and seek rules and actions that do as much as possible for all involved. Our country needs a certain number of immigrants, and I feel very badly for people in other countries who have terrible lives through no fault of their own. I'm all for admitting as many immigrants as we can without causing our laws and social structures to slowly dissolve.

Other Opinions

(one view) We don't need countries any more. They just get in the way of daily life. Anyone who wants to should be allowed to live here (or anywhere else, for that matter). If we truly want to be a multicultural society, then it doesn't matter how many of which kind of people we have, and everyone should be able to have whatever beliefs and customs they bring with them.

(another view) We shouldn't have immigrants at all because they just take jobs that Americans need. Besides, they are offensive and don't belong here.

"THE WALL"

The idea of effective protection of the country via a wall between Mexico and the U.S. is an illusion—an attractive illusion, but still an illusion. The history of arms races is that neither side gives up but instead seeks better methods to defeat the other. Any wall can be tunneled under, blown up, etc., and people can simply walk through all gaps in the wall, anyway, or come into the country at another place or by sea. (Mr. Trump did not propose to build a continuous wall all the way along our southern border, anyway.) If there is a wall in south Texas, smugglers will land more people along Texas' Gulf of Mexico coast. Fencing is useful at some points along the border, but an impregnable wall is largely a waste of money. (These words should not be construed as a subtle support for illegal immigration, which I strongly oppose.)

Other Opinions

We've got to stop illegal immigration, and a wall is one way to do it. We should build a wall all the way around our country (Canada, too), no matter how much it costs. Allowing volunteer bands of vigilantes to patrol along the border, empowered to shoot anyone coming in illegally, would be effective, too.

OTHER ISSUES INVOLVING GOVERNMENT

FREE SPEECH

Almost all of us want to be able to express our opinions freely, without fear of punishment, and in general this should be protected. The only reason to prohibit speech in a democracy is if it harms others. It cannot be acceptable to restrict speech solely because it questions or criticizes leaders or political groups. On the other hand, we have already made some speech punishable (libel, slander, inciting riot, advocating overthrow of the government by force, human stampede), and we may wish to seriously consider extending that to include other harms that speech can cause. There is concern among parents about on-line bullying, for instance, where speech can in some cases lead to emotional problems or even suicide in children (although this is likely only in participants who are already unusually emotionally vulnerable). Some young people want to be protected from speech that upsets them ("safe spaces"). Many people prefer not to listen to a great deal of profanity in others' speech, though while this would be offensive, it is generally not harmful.

For the sake of having healthy and meaningful dialogue among citizens that will strengthen our democracy, I believe that the appropriate compromise at the moment on the issue of free speech is to allow all speech except that which directly aims to harm and which a "reasonable person" would perceive correctly to be potentially directly harmful to many others. Many times, there are alternatives to censoring speech. Parents can protect children from on-line bullying by not allowing them to use the internet outlets involved or by giving their children more emotional support. People can group or gather only with others who will not speak in ways that upset them (although that will unfortunately tend to create groups in society who cannot talk to each other). People can stop using internet outlets where they are hearing too much profanity. Currently our internet outlets are private companies who will only change if enough users walk away from them. If we had government social media outlets, then government would be setting and enforcing standards.

Other Opinions

If I want to express myself aggressively or profanely, that should be my right. Why do I have to talk like you? Getting the country's business right is too important to justify cutting off any input that citizens have. "If it's too hot in the kitchen, get out of the kitchen!"

PRIVACY

In accord with human needs for feeling secure and valued, we have a definite need for a sense of personal privacy, so that certain aspects of our thoughts and behavior can be protected from exposure to others. This must be balanced with society's need to be able to know enough about our thoughts and behaviors that others can feel secure and valued as well, as well as with the need of society to be able to investigate and correct illegal behavior. Our greater mobility and anonymity (travel, frequent moving, being unknown to neighbors, using false identities on the internet) have enabled people to lie to and steal from others in ways not even conceived of before (internet scams, cryptocurrency scams, identity theft, losing oneself in a crowd), and it is an axiom that the more power we have over others individually (to harm others, by making bombs at home, invading others' privacy, etc.), the more society will insist on knowing our business. *This is a difficult intersection of "rights" to work out, and in my opinion it requires intense and deep discussions. I will institute and participate in these discussions.*

Another aspect of this intersection is the desire of many people to know others' business, even when their own security and value are not threatened—viz., the gossip industry targeting celebrities of various sorts and well as anyone whose life story could make a salable story, movie, or expose. It is natural for human beings to want to know enough about others to be able to anticipate others' behavior and therefore protect themselves, but this legitimate interest often shades over into *a desire to know that is for purposes of feeling superior or to have power over others. This is not a healthy pursuit, and I will not help to legitimize or encourage such efforts.*

A third aspect of the privacy concern is the obtaining and sale of personal data, which is the primary source of income for internet companies and which provides buyers of such data opportunity to "target" communications to us that will be maximally effective in getting us to buy or do certain things (or to vote certain ways). The data is collected by granting us use of "free" elements of the internet (shopping, email, other apps, etc.)—anything for which we need to agree to terms and conditions of service in order to use—only if we agree to have our data stored and shared, by checking a box, almost always without reading those terms and conditions. *I have a strong aversion to this stockpiling of personal data, by business or government, and I will seek to curtail such stockpiling and prohibit its use. The use of this data for manipulation takes away an individual's opportunity to make the best decisions he/she can to take care of oneself, and as such is a harm.*

CLIMATE CHANGE AND OTHER GLOBAL PROBLEMS

I believe that nations must cooperate in as many ways as possible on issues that affect all nations, including global climate change and global trade. I will utilize all effective means of encouraging and participating in this cooperation, including activity in the United Nations and other global groups, without ceding any of our rights to protect United States interests. These efforts will not be short-sighted efforts to gain advantage for this country at the expense of others in the world but will seek reasonable and fair outcomes that build a cooperative and trusting climate for future negotiations and problem-solving.

It seems clear that human activity does contribute to the natural warming cycle that the earth is undergoing right now. You can't burn fuels without creating heat, and there are now billions of us doing it. This could be ignored when human populations were small, but now with eight billion people we are doing enough heating to make a difference in the world's weather. The more important focus, though, should be what we should be doing to prepare our nation for expectable changes, such as rising sea levels and soil temperatures, and to ensure that we change crops to those that can thrive in slightly warmer temperatures. It doesn't seem realistic that we can have enough green energy to completely replace burning fuels (what about back-up power generation when the sun doesn't shine and the wind doesn't blow?), but we should build as much green energy infrastructure as we can. As noted elsewhere, the vain hope of bringing resources to Earth from the moon or Mars is foolish, since the price will always be out of reach.

We must balance taking steps to change over to green power as much as possible with the pain this is causing to consumers and to businesses. Transitions that are too fast or abrupt create more resistance. Another balancing issue regarding climate is whether we feel responsibility to future generations to maintain a livable planet. Most of us would prefer to maintain a livable planet, but for most of us this must be at a reasonable cost to those now living. *I will continue to encourage green energy enterprise but at a slightly slower pace, to accommodate the needs of our citizens.*

Other Opinions
Every nation is out for itself, so none can be trusted. We should be as self-sufficient as possible. Even though we are seeing weather extremes right now, that doesn't prove that global warming is happening or that it wouldn't happen in nearly the same way without our contributions.

Fossil Fuels
If we are to limit the rise in world temperature (which will cause some species on the planet to go extinct and will require us to change the grains that we grow to fit the new temperatures), we will have to stop burning as much as we burn. Our heating, our electricity, our cars, and many industrial processes operate mostly by burning oil or gas and converting the resultant heat to our purposes, but there is always heat loss into the atmosphere. Every time you operate your computer, it puts out a tiny bit of heat, and when we multiply that tiny bit by the number of computers in the world, it is no longer negligible but contributes to the global heat increase. (We are used to simply ignoring many of these contributions to heat, but now that there are so many of us and we want so much more energy use, it all adds up to something significant.)

The main thrust of the efforts to control global temperature center around making more of the energy we want using solar panels, wind turbines, and, in the future, tidal power. We are trying to convert to depending on these sources, all of which have some disadvantages, like the fact that when clouds cover the sun, there is less energy generated by solar panels, so the conversion is challenging. We may always need some non-environmentally-friendly source, like gas powered power plants, as backup. The world is making surprisingly great progress in this regard, although countries vary a lot in how hard they are working on this, and poor countries, in general, are changing the least. Our country is already committed to making the change, but we must balance that change against the prices of energy that our citizens are paying. I believe that we are going too fast with restricting gas and coal production from our own sources, which is done partly to boost private investment in eco-friendly methods but is also increasing current energy prices to consumers. *I will be more inclined than the current administration to keep more of our own fossil fuel drilling and exploration going, and slow down the changeover a bit.*

Other Opinions

We've got to press on with the changeover. Every day we tarry, some other species goes extinct and our future average temperatures go up a bit. That is worth paying for.

POPULATION

We do not need more children! Our global population of eight billion is straining the capacity of the worldwide economy to deliver even enough food for us all to survive, let alone other consumer goods to help third-world countries improve the lives of their citizens. Did you know that twenty to twenty-five percent of the world's people are currently dependent on aid (charity from the rest of the world, like the U.N., Oxfam, etc.) to live, including in refugee and displaced person camps? The tide of immigration to the U.S. and to Europe includes many who cannot maintain human life where they are currently living—they must move or die.

It is one our instinctual functions to have sex and therefore inevitably produce babies, and it is instinctual for human females (somewhat more than males) to care for these babies. This keeps our species alive, but *we are reaching a point of enough crowding and few enough remaining resources that wars and diseases are likely to take over the job of limiting the human population. In order to avoid this, sooner or later we will have to do some limiting of our reproduction.* China tried this (one-child per couple policy), which didn't work out well because of the Chinese cultural bias toward males (leaving many female babies to die instead of grow, so that now many males can't find female partners). More education and jobs for women has had a slowing effect on population, and there may be other changes that have positive results and at the same time slow population growth. Reproductive rates in developed countries will need to be lowered in order to incorporate the over-reproduction in less developed countries!

Businesses always forecast that we will need an increasing number of workers in the future, but this assumes that we wish to keep on growing, and our over-population problem dictates that we stop growing or at least grow only as much as can be accommodated without further damage to resources and environment.

Reproduction is so fundamental to our notions about living that it will be very difficult to agree on policies that could limit population, like a two-children only policy, tax penalties for having more than two children (instead of tax help for having more children), no childcare reimbursement for more than two children, or an expectation of surgical sterilization of both males and females after a certain age or after having their two children, but if we don't act, then sooner or later people will start fighting each other for basic resources. Many have a blind faith that science and technology will stay ahead of those eventualities, but science and technology have their limits (just as human knowledge has ultimate limits), and given our human tendency to always want more and to eliminate any discomfort that we have, sooner or later, we will use up the findable resources in the world. The myth of getting resources from the moon or Mars is foolish, since the costs of doing it are insurmountable.

With more people we would need more and more power, and every power generation method uses up or changes some of the world's resources. Wind power changes the patterns of global wind (and therefore global weather). Solar power reduces the sun's warming of the planet, which will affect heat patterns in the interior of the earth and therefore affect volcanic activity. Tidal power changes the movements of the earth's ocean currents and therefore our weather. There is no free lunch. We can either keep the number of people on the earth in balance with these resource and environment factors (at least enough to slow the rate of draining of all resources by half or more) or overpopulate and suffer the consequences of that. *I will organize and promote the beginning of discussions on this topic, since it will take a lot of discussion to start to bring society to the point of taking any action on this topic!*

Other Opinions

Again, you are exaggerating. There's lots of land left, and science and technology will still be making our lives better for at least a little while longer. If we are inevitably going to destroy ourselves with atomic bombs, why bother about any of this? The world's remaining poor deserve a chance at a comfortable life, and you would take that away from them with your policies.

INFRASTRUCTURE

Our infrastructure (public facilities such as water systems, sewer systems, roads, bridges flood levees) is aging and increasingly subject to breakdown (recently, water in Jackson MS and Flint MI, a bridge in Minnesota). We think of these items as something given to us without cost, presumably forever, but this is inaccurate. Someone built them before our time, at considerable cost, but *it is up to us to keep them functioning well*. Citizens don't want to have to do this, since it entails cost, but we must take care of it. Instead of dealing with these things as separate incidents, *I think we should have a comprehensive plan, with a schedule for checking on and correcting problems, and I will lead the development of such a comprehensive system.*

Cost responsibility should be at the lowest possible level—i.e., a local water or sewer system should be paid for by those local communities, just as the money for the interstate highway system is borne by the federal government. Towns and cities always try to get someone else to pay for these things, but it is their responsibility to pay, and taxing decisions must be made to take care of this. This will mean a slowing of growth and a decrement in standard of living, but it simply must be done, and it's better to get ahead of the game than wait until some essential unit or service completely breaks down before we act. *It would be in everyone's best interest to have a long term savings plan for these expenses, so that when a need arises, at least part of the money is already gathered.* Of course, this notion of savings is so out of fashion, on the part of individuals and at all levels of government that it will take some will power to reestablish it and protect those monies from being diverted to use for other short-term needs. Citizens should have a greater sense of personal and group responsibility for such projects.

Other Opinions
No one will take a tax hit to pay for public services, since they always think that someone else should pay for it. People will only respond to crises, so we have to just let them happen.

SOCIAL SECURITY

The Social Security program has served a useful purpose in providing both disability assistance (SSDI) and retirement income to Americans. Not enough is coming into the program through current payroll deductions to ensure a healthy fund, and this must be corrected soon. *I will press*

Congress to amend the fund's legislation immediately to keep income sufficient to pay expected responsibilities in the future.

In addition, since the fund was designed to provide bare bones amounts for both disability and retirement, *I will work toward adding a companion program to enhance the retirement income payouts.* This will be managed through the current Social Security Administration, using payroll deductions, and it will be optional for contributors who can also set the amount of their contributions to this new program. This will provide a more adequate retirement income for people through long-term savings, which seems difficult for many citizens to do using their own motivation (since we encourage them to spend as consumers rather than save).

Other Opinions

All citizens should pay for the disability program, not just those contributing to the Social Security fund. Retirement savings should be the responsibility of each citizen. We should abolish Social Security and let Americans use the stock market to leverage their savings as possible for retirement income.

FINANCIAL ACCOUNTABILITY

While there is a tradition of government functionaries not being subject to lawsuit for financial decisions, *I will press for legislation permitting civil and criminal charges against government employees who spend inappropriately or fail to stop inappropriate spending through their own neglect or malfeasance.* In other words, if they clearly were trying to spend or authorize spending to benefit themselves or other individuals, they should pay in court, including repayment of some of the lost monies. Similarly, I will seek to have financial institution managers and employees prosecuted for engaging in investments that they know are risky without telling investors exactly the risk or without proof of investor authorization to proceed. (The quarterly reports that investment firms currently send to investors for each holding will not suffice for this! Brokers and investment managers must take more personal responsibility for their actions.) It will be illegal to create investment packages for which the risk cannot be estimated with reasonable certainty, as this is largely what led to the financial downturn of 2008.

Other Opinions

If Congresspersons and other government officials have to risk some of their own money betting on the things they pass or enforce, no one will run for office or work for the government.

PORK

It has been traditional for Congresspersons to get money for their constituents, thereby showing what a good job they are doing. This turns every district into a competitor with other districts to get that pork. *If there is to be such a thing as Congresspersons getting monies just for their own districts, I will advocate that a total pool of money for this be decided on by Congress, and then advocate that every district get the same per-person amount.*

Other Opinions

My voters don't care about any other voters in the country. They just want me to help them by getting more money for them.

MERIT HIRING (NO SPOILS)

In the best interest of all citizens, *all positions within the government will be filled according to merit (experience, competence, leadership ability, etc.), including the President's cabinet and all ambassadorships, rather than as a spoils system that rewards people who have helped and supported me.* People should not contribute to my campaign with the hope of personal gain, either in terms of employment or influence, since I will not honor such requests. *I will attempt to influence Congress to fill its committee positions on the basis of merit as well, rather than on the basis of seniority and political affiliation.*

This anti-spoils-system philosophy extends to financial contributors to my campaign. *All contributors are being informed through this book and website information of my positions and agenda and will be informed that their contributions will further this work as stated. They should only contribute if they want the kind of government that I will provide. Their contributions will not give their wishes or views any more weight than the weight given to the wishes and views of non-contributors.* All citizens are encouraged to seek individual help from the government regarding the fair and appropriate application to them individually of the laws and regulations of this country, and whether or not such an individual voted for me or contributed to my campaign will not be asked or recorded and will have no bearing on the help provided to them.

Other Opinions

Promising campaign contributors influence in government, job positions, or ambassadorships are so much a part of our system, we have to keep it up. Otherwise they won't contribute to our campaigns.

SUPREME COURT

Blaming the judiciary for "legislating from the bench" is simply a way for legislators to divert attention from the fact that they have not done their legislative job well. Judges attempt to interpret the law as written when the law is unclear, and when necessary the Supreme Court interprets the Constitution as it applies to the law being considered. I will push legislators to do their full jobs as legislators by rewriting and clarifying the laws (or seeking to amend the Constitution), rather than passing the buck to the courts. When Supreme Court decisions are clearly at odds with the preferences of the people in general, constitutional amendments should be sought. We should keep clear in our minds that it is not the job of the Supreme Court to decide whether something is "right" but only whether it violates the law (e.g., the Court does not decide whether abortion is morally right or wrong, but only how abortion is affected by our existing laws).

Ideas about our democracy have changed since the Constitution was written, so much so that "originalist" judges in the Supreme Court insist that we try to understand what the framers meant by what they wrote instead of "reinterpreting" what they wrote to fit today's environment. The mere fact that we must make the effort to do that shows that we do not readily understand what the framers meant and could very well get it wrong in our current efforts, since individuals (even judges) tend to think that their own framework of understanding things must be or should be universal and therefore that what they think the framers meant must be what they meant. This proves that we need a Constitutional Convention to clarify all of the assumptions made by Congress and the courts about what our Constitution "means." This is too important an issue to leave it to a few individuals instead of the whole body politic.

The concept of Republicans and Democrats each trying to appoint people to the Court who will reliably vote conservative or liberal is anathema to justice and fairness, and both parties should be ashamed of themselves for doing this. Justice should always be reasonable and in the best interest of the country as a whole. There are still many people in our country who can set aside their own views and biases in order to do what is right and lawful, and Supreme Court justices should be appointed from this group. *I will nominate to the Supreme Court only persons who think independently about judicial matters and who demonstrate the ability to consider the law objectively even when in some instances that goes against their own political philosophy.*

Other Opinions

Yes, we pass bills that are ambiguous, because no one will compromise enough for us to pass anything detailed. We can only pass on the details to the bureaucracies that carry out the law or to the courts. The game of fighting over conservative vs. liberal concepts in the Supreme Court is just the same as the fighting in Congress, so why shouldn't we be doing it? Having a Constitutional Convention would make more trouble than it would solve, so we are better off bumbling along as we are currently doing.

UNRELATED AMENDMENTS TO BILLS IN CONGRESS

The practice by legislative bodies of freely allowing their members to add (by vote) amendments to bills that have nothing to do with those bills (usually to appropriate money for another purpose or address some totally unrelated issue) has produced much harm and little good, since it either hides the purpose of the amendment from public view or leads to the defeat of the original bill (the "poison pill" amendment). This practice continues largely so that members can do exactly these things. *I will push Congress to prohibit the practice of unrelated amendments and instead ensure that bills address only a single issue.* Those unrelated amendments can be considered as separate bills, to stand or fall on their own merit.

Other Opinions

If we eliminate unrelated amendments, then a lot of little things, like a commendation for some individual, won't get done. There's just too much to do. If we couldn't tack on unrelated amendments, we could never get anything for our own districts, since the other Congresspersons don't care about our districts, and we don't care about theirs. The Speakers of the House and Senate would never put our one-item bills for our own districts to a vote; there's not enough time to do that.

UP OR DOWN VOTES ON ALL BILLS

Currently, the Majority Party only "allows" the House or Senate to vote on certain bills—the usual practice being not to vote unless the Majority Party thinks it can "win." This deprives the voters of knowing what Congress is doing and prevents public opinion from forming around the issue in question. *I will advocate for a vote (called an "up or down" vote) on every bill that goes through the vetting process Congress uses. Alternatively, the House and the Senate should have a rule that any member can request a vote by that chamber on whether to open debate on a particular bill, with a majority vote resulting in consideration of that bill.* There is no reason not to vote on it and then attempt to re-introduce the same bill or a bill that will get more approval. In order to do this, the power of the Speakers of the House and Senate will have to be reduced. The President does not have the power to make Congressional procedure rules, but I will highlight to the public the negative impact of the Speakers having so much power. (The huge amount of time Congresspersons spend asking for contributions to their next campaigns should be converted into more time to read the bills being voted on by having base levels of election funding for qualified candidates paid for by the government!)

Other Opinions
There is much maneuvering that goes on as bills are altered and rejected or approved at various levels. We don't want to cut down on this maneuvering by having up-or-down votes, and we don't want voters to know how we would vote on certain controversial issues, so we just don't vote on them.

BIG STATES VS. SMALL STATES

To ensure that the original, larger colonies (in population) would not dominate the smaller colonies inappropriately, our Constitution gave some voting advantages to small states, giving them the same representation in the Senate as the larger states and a slightly larger say in who is elected President. It is important to maintain some self-protective power for smaller states, but given the change in loyalties over the life of our country, that balance should probably be adjusted. No one any more would say that they were "a Virginian" before they were an American. So, apportionment should follow the meaning of whatever vote is at issue.

Americans all think of the President as the President of all citizens equally, not as an arbiter among powerful states, so the Presidential vote should be by popular vote of the entire country. *The representation of smaller states in the Senate should probably still give a bit more say to smaller states, but it should be more like 1.5 votes per smaller state instead of two votes* (two Senators). This change is unlikely to happen in my tenure, but this simply shows how much we need a Constitutional Convention, to rewrite and clarify our Constitution.

Other Opinions
Smaller States: Our Constitution is sacred and its framers were geniuses, so it should not be meddled with. We like the power we have, and if we didn't have it, we would become second class states.

Larger States; We are shackled with the often backward and parochial views of smaller states. Let's have the Convention!

FEDERAL VS. STATES

We have an ongoing uneasy détente between the Federal government and the fifty states. States sometimes complain about intrusion and control by the Feds (by Congress and by agencies) and say that they want to determine more things for themselves, but they generally continue to want as much Federal monies as possible, in effect wanting to use Federal taxes for state purposes instead of raising state taxes. This, however, ties them to dependence on the Federal government! Congress, on the other hand, seeking power as many politicians and political groups do, is happy to keep the states dependent on the money they can hand out. This is not a healthy relationship and will never be until states are more willing to support themselves (telling their citizens what things cost and where their state taxes are going and citizens being willing to pay for what they want). (It is a strange paradox that the representatives of the states and their citizens in Congress are the ones to decide whether to "intrude" on the rights of the states by exerting Federal control, yet they consistently move to be more dependent on the Federal government!)

Much of the tension between the Federal and state governments is due to the fact that some issues are better dealt with by the states separately while some affect the union of states so much that Federal solutions must take precedence over state solutions. Take the difference between states wanting to control school curriculums for their children and the Congress wanting them to emphasize STEM areas more since it seems to be important to our technological prowess and therefore to our GDP. The states aren't worried about the GDP, but the Feds may believe that they must exert control in this matter because the ultimate outcome will affect all states financially, including those that don't care about STEM training.

We should deal with each of these kinds of issues separately as they come along. It should not be a matter of who has more power and control (the state or the Feds) but of how the issue will affect people at all levels. If we all care about the concerns of all of our fellow citizens, then we will want to understand why different groups and different states want what they want, and following this understanding, we must work together (states and "the Feds," and those representing the states in our Congress) to find the solution that benefits the most and disadvantages the fewest. The key is an attitude of cooperation and expecting that everyone's views will be honored and responded to as much as possible.

Other Opinions

Since it is the nature of people in government to want more power, and since the Federal government ultimately has more power than the states, all of us must look with a jaundiced eye at every Federal law and regulation that directly affects each of our states. We must resist every intrusion in order to keep as much of a balance as possible.

Unfunded Mandates

UNFUNDED MANDATES

It is inappropriate for any legislating or rule-making body to order all bodies below itself to carry out certain behaviors that are for the benefit of the ordering body only, without providing funds to pay for the required actions. Thus, it is inappropriate for Congress to pass legislation requiring all the states to carry out certain reporting/data functions that are primarily for the benefit of Congress and other federal agencies without paying the states to collect and provide that information. It is certainly simpler for Congress to require it but not pay for it, but it leads to greater irresponsibility of Congress the more it engages in such actions. Every governmental action costs money, and the level of government that primarily benefits should pay for that action. I realize that this may complicate things for Congress, but honesty and responsibility should be required for everyone at all levels.

Other Opinions
The body above has the power to order things without paying, so why shouldn't they? Everybody is out to get the most for themselves, even Congress.

OFFICIAL LANGUAGE

A nation cannot efficiently conduct its business without a uniform language in which to conduct that business. Citizens may use any language they wish for private purposes, but there should be no obligation for government or businesses to conduct business in languages other than English. This does not imply that English is a superior language or that English-speakers should have more rights than others. It is chosen simply because it is the majority language currently. Having a standard language that all citizens learn will benefit all citizens through better communications and is a key aspect of identification of all citizens with the nation. There are countries which have made a dual-language society "work" (Canada, Ireland), but it is expensive and never eliminates the conflict over which culture's language to favor and how to ensure even distribution of resources.

Other Opinions
Every group and every language should have equal value, and therefore all should be equally acceptable. We can be a multi-language society, just as some other countries are.

A CONSTITUTIONAL CONVENTION

People ignore the possibility of having a Constitutional Convention because it takes so many states to approve any changes made, but we badly need to clarify and to change some things in our Constitution, including some election issues, as noted above. Having the Convention would stimulate creative thinking about how we want our country to work, and it would eliminate some of the need for the Supreme Court to "interpret" what the Founding Fathers intended. We should not pretend that our Founding Fathers were fortune tellers who could see every possible governmental difficulty that could arise in the future. Having such a Convention will raise the level of uncertainty for both individuals and businesses, but I believe that the creative outcomes of the Convention will settle many more problems than it causes, especially over time. *I will begin the process of gathering ideas about necessary topics for such a Convention and of convincing Congress to make one happen.*

Other Opinions

No matter what we do or change, there will still be difficulties in how our government functions. We are managing the way things are now, so we should just let things be rather than risking making mistakes in our further decisions.

ELECTION ISSUES

MY APPROACH TO ELECTIONS

Since an educated and informed electorate is essential to a healthy democracy, my appeals to voters will be structured to educate voters about how I understand the country's problems and what I would do to solve them. This information will be conveyed honestly and with integrity, as well as with due respect for the positions of other groups. These communications will be sufficient in detail to explain the pros and cons of each position, instead of presenting only one side of things. Every solution to a public problem has negative consequences as well as the intended positive consequences. There is no perfect solution for any of the problems we face. Therefore, in my communications *I will always include a response to the key disagreements that some might have with my position.* This principle will apply also to all interviews by the press – if the answer or position will not be represented adequately in the press (in sufficient detail to educate), the interview will not be given. "Sound-bites" and short appeals to voter emotions will not be used by me. Interviews that are only for the purpose of filling time in newscasts will not be given. (The principle, of also addressing the less desirable consequences of any position, should also be a requirement, in my opinion, for editorials and op-ed pieces in the media.)

Other Opinions
People vote on emotion, so to get elected you must sneak in on their emotions regardless of the facts. Our press, biased as it may be, is our biggest source of information about politics for the voters, so we need to keep it stoked up so they will vote.

MOTIVES OF CANDIDATES

My prime motive is to set up our elections so that the best qualified candidate will be elected, rather than the most popular. *If I become convinced that another candidate is better qualified than I, I will swing my support to that candidate and end my own campaign.* As stated already, integrity and the welfare of the nation must be the most important values in voting, rather than a candidate's desire to be in a certain office or position. Candidates should compete on the basis of their ideas and plans, should not appeal only to part of the electorate, and should not promise to give advantage to some citizens over others. It is not possible to continue to take advantage of others over time and not experience the same from them eventually, and a political atmosphere of respect, consideration, and cooperation will produce better results for each segment of society and for humanity in general than a competition for who can take advantage of others best through raw power, unholy alliances, or secret deals.

Many candidates are unfortunately motivated by a secret wish for power. Those who think it natural and inevitable that most politicians want power should take caution from the fact that those politicians want power over *them* personally, not just power in general. The thrill of power is that one can gain benefit for oneself by controlling others, so politicians motivated by power really do want to feel power over you personally – the power to determine certain aspects of your life for *their* advantage. The alternative to allowing those who seek power to govern must be to *give the power of political position only to those who do not want that power to control and have no wish to control you or your life – those who instead want to help you to do what you want for your life.* Those who seek the thrill of power and wish to use political position to further their own interests regardless of the impact on others are a danger to you and to the nation and should be prohibited from gaining this kind of power. Other useful things for them to do must be found – e.g., positions of authority in which we want power to be exercised directly but limited by appropriate rules, such as in the justice system and the military. Tolerating the manipulative behavior of those who base their lives on taking advantage of others, whether that is in politics or car sales, reduces the wealth and happiness of all other citizens. (The maxim "let the buyer beware" describes, unfortunately, what actually happens in our society. It should not be a standard for sellers' behavior!)

Another class of politician is motivated largely by the wish for fame and adulation. These people do not necessarily want power over you, but they will do whatever they believe will get them fame and adulation, rather than what is good for the country. If we are to prosper, we sometimes need politicians who will do what is good for the country even if that sometimes goes against the opinion of many voters, such as *not* spending more and *not* increasing the national debt even though we might all like the benefits of what that immediate overspending could give us. Politicians motivated by fame and adulation cannot make these "hard decisions" in the best long-term interest of the nation because it is unnatural for them to do so.

Some voters are swayed by candidates who seem powerful or who say they will "fight for" the voter. Certainly there are some times when the country needs a strong President, but this fighting privileges some and disadvantages others, and a powerful person can always turn that power on you! It is critical that voters attend during elections to who can do the job best and particularly to eliminating candidates who seek personal power.

Other Opinions

Americans are always out for themselves (take care of #1, Baby), so it's fine that candidates want to be elected for their own personal gratification and benefit.

TERM LIMITS

Because most politicians are motivated more by self-interest than by service to the country, term limits will allow them to forget their long-term careers and do a better job for the country. Term limits should be something like House-three terms (six years), Senate-two terms (twelve years), President-two terms (eight years), and Supreme Court-one term (twenty years). Having more than one term for all offices allows for some familiarity with the job to build up in the first term and be useful in the second and later terms. There is something to be said for continuity in office, but the negative effects of having to continue to be elected for a whole career outweigh the positives effects of continuity.

COUNTING VOTES

We have a tradition of simply counting votes for each candidate and declaring the one with the most votes the winner ("winner-take-all"). In some jurisdictions the final winner must have more than fifty percent of the vote, which may require a "run-off" election between the top two candidates. Another option would be what is called "preferential" vote-counting, in which voters mark a first choice, a second choice, a third choice, etc., instead of just voting for one candidate. In some types of preferential voting, at each stage of the preferential vote-counting, several of the bottom candidates are eliminated and voters who marked them number one have their votes reassigned to the candidates they had marked as second, third, etc. This process continues until there is a winner with more than fifty percent of the vote. *I favor this preferential model of voting, since it allows voters to give more information about who they want in office.*

Other Opinions
This would just confuse voters. We have a perfectly good system now, so let's keep it.

GERRYMANDERING

Reassigning voting district boundaries is only permissible for equalizing population in each district, so that representation is equal per thousand citizens. Efforts by the two major parties to design districts to advantage themselves is reprehensible and should be illegal. The use of non-partisan commissions to do the (for most states) every ten-year redesign is more desirable than having the state legislature do it. Effort should be made to have districts include the same proportion of voters as those who are registered in the state to the two major parties, so that there will be no "safe" seats that parties can count on to win.

The courts should have a final say as to inappropriate boundaries, based on two concepts. (1) The more a district deviates from a regular form that is more or less round or square (as opposed to strangely elongated), the more likely it is to be an inappropriate manipulation. (2) A district that does not reflect the general percentages of various groups in the state (by race, income, educational level, etc.) is more likely to be inappropriate. Of necessity, some districts will violate one or both of these criteria, but the whole pattern must look reasonably appropriate.

I realize that these criteria act against creating districts that are almost certain to elect a Black person (or a white person or a Latino person...) in order to guarantee those groups some representation, but I think the better approach is to make representing everyone equally the key to being elected, by creating truly contestable districts.

Other Opinions

America is the land of competition, and the parties should be able to fight to the max, including by changing districts to benefit themselves. It is good press to create Black districts, as long as there are not too many of them.

MAKING IT HARD OR EASY TO VOTE

Making it difficult or impossible for a citizen to vote through various tests or requirements, as was done in the South during and after Reconstruction, should be (and is) illegal, but it is appropriate to have measures in place to ensure that a person is a legitimate voter (that the person is a citizen over a certain age and resides in the district). Allowing anyone to walk in and vote (or vote by mail) just because they are present in the district on election day or just because they send in a card, is too open, unless voter registration requires incontrovertible proof before registration and this can somehow be confirmed again at the time of voting (such as by a thumbprint rather than a signature). Whatever means are used, they cannot be more stringent than proof of citizenship and residence.

Most of the requirements for voting instituted by states after the 2016 election were not unduly burdening for voters, even though the liberal press made it seem that they were. Requiring voters, for instance, to have a state-issued ID card might make it more difficult for a few voters, but this could be corrected by offering home visits by officials to get the card just by calling or e-mailing. Not allowing political parties to hand out water to voters waiting to vote may have sounded ridiculous, but handing out water (or baseball caps, or bobble-head dolls, cash, or whatever) would be a way for a political party to sway voters in their direction at the last minute, and this cannot be allowed during the voting process.

CAMPAIGNS

Most campaigns are designed to appeal to enough voters to gain a win but not to appeal to all voters. I believe that campaigns should present who the candidate is and what he/she will strive to do if elected. Everything else (billboards, TV ads, rallies) is attempted manipulation. Candidates should then see how many voters favor them and their ideas, and the person with the most votes wins. Candidates should be satisfied with the will of the people, and the will of the people is really indeterminate if the voters don't know who they are voting for and end up voting for the manipulation that appeals the most to them (appealing to their prejudices and emotions). *We could construct a questionnaire that would help us get a sense of each candidate (attitudes about service, attitudes about power, willingness to compromise, willingness to serve all the people and not just one side, integrity, morals, etc., as well intentions if in office as seen in this document).* Candidates' answers to these questionnaires could be distributed to all voters. (Yes, candidates could lie, but I think that overall the American people can tell lies from truth if they want to.)

The length of our campaigning is making seeking office almost a full-time activity! There is no rational advantage to this for purposes of electing the best qualified candidate. It only gives all candidates more time to try to manipulate voters. *I will support limiting campaigns to six months, as that is plenty of time to tell voters who you are and what you stand for.*

The desire to win shows in all campaign manipulations (including lying on the above questionnaires), as ads are constructed to be misleading rather than informative and truthful. It won't be long before some campaign pays to have false videos made (deep fakes) that depict opponents saying things that they have never said. These fakes (another product of our facial recognition push) will be very hard for voters to detect—just another indicator of lack of integrity.

Other Opinions

Campaigns that are big fights to win serve the people best because the people want to find someone who will be a winner as President. Why shouldn't this be the candidate who can fight the best? All's fair in love and war! People want a winner who is the strongest. They don't care much about morals or integrity.

ELECTORAL COSTS

Elections in this country have become extremely expensive, due largely to the costs of competing via TV ads, and contributing money to support candidates or issues has largely replaced actual expression of political views by voters, which is a dangerous precedent. (Free speech should be actual speech. Giving money shows support, but it is not speech.) Many voters contribute to campaigns because they are afraid that if they don't, then the other candidate will get more contributions and will win the election. This swells the total monies used for the campaigns but to no good purpose. If we all stopped contributing out of fear of being left behind, it would reduce total spending a great deal. The huge amount of spending also makes competing with the two major political parties almost impossible for smaller groups. *I will work to promote public funding for candidates (though still allowing other, separate organizations to accept donations to be used for publicity on issues rather than candidates.* (The difficulty, of course, will be defining who is included as a "candidate.") I am not trying to reduce free speech but to make free speech more efficient by making speakers consider more carefully what they have to say.)

I will support public funding for only those campaign and election practices that support a healthy democracy (information for voters about candidates' qualifications and characteristics; information for voters about issues) and will discourage those practices that subvert democracy (lying and deception through advertising; limiting the information available to voters; negative advertising; appealing to voters' prejudices; etc.). Information produced with the support of public funding will be subject to the lying/deception misdemeanor limitations described elsewhere. *As a candidate I will provide voters with an analysis of opponents' ads, showing you how they try to deceive you.*

Secondly, *I will work to ensure that no expenses for party primary elections are paid for with our taxes.* Parties should pay all the expenses of primary elections, which are useful only for the parties themselves. Let them go back to having conventions. (This is an example of how political parties have entwined themselves so thoroughly in government that citizens think that the parties must be required aspects of elections.)

Other Opinions

Campaign costs are astronomical, of course, but the answer isn't to restrict campaign spending, because the competition for monetary support is a good indicator of the will of the people. Yes, all that money could be used for benefiting the people, but then how are you going to get it? People don't want to give money to help the country or help people who are having it hard! If people want to elect a liar or a convicted felon, then they have the right to do that.

PRESIDENT TRUMP

Looking carefully at Mr. Trump's history and expressions has led me to conclude that he is in politics not for the sake of any segment of society but for his own power and fame. He promised to represent a highly conservative, disillusioned segment of society that felt ignored and left behind by society, but he did little or nothing to benefit them after he was elected. I agree with his two major actions—pressing NATO countries to pay their fair share and pressing China to play by international trade rules, and he had some success in those two areas. His tax reduction was presented as if it would be in the best interest of middle and lower classes, but it led to a ballooning national debt that those same middle and lower class voters will have to pay off as they get older (not the best long-term policy). I am very concerned about his willingness to ignore or try to get around the laws of our country, since this is certainly destructive to our democracy. I don't want a strong-arm man as my President, and that's what he aspires to be.

Other Opinions

No one else is doing anything right in Washington, so we need someone strong enough to force them to do better, even if means ignoring some of our laws. Mr. Trump at least told us (those disillusioned and left behind) that it was not our fault and that our values were worthwhile.

FOREIGN RELATIONS AND FOREIGN POLICY

I believe that nations must cooperate in as many ways as possible on issues that affect all nations, including global climate change and global trade. I will utilize all effective means of encouraging and participating in this cooperation, including activity in the United Nations and other global groups, without ceding any of our rights to protect United States interests. These efforts will not be short-sighted efforts to gain advantage for this country at the expense of others in the world but will seek reasonable and fair outcomes that build a cooperative and trusting climate for future negotiations and problem-solving.

WORLD PEACE

The idea of world peace is an important aspiration for all of us who reject any and all stealing of land or goods from one country by another. Border intrusions are always wrong if unprovoked. Defending one's country is of course OK, but aggression is not.

Leaders of countries are prime villains in the creation of wars, since most citizens of all countries would rather not fight and die in an unnecessary war. Leaders who lead toward war want to be heroes and demonstrate their power, and this always leads to citizen deaths. Citizens in all countries should become more discerning about whom they elect, and keep out of office all leaders who are thin-skinned and who aspire to power. We should pay more attention to organizations that promote world peace, such as the United Nations, the Quakers of the world, and the Peace and Social Justice section of the American Psychological Association, the members of which do research about causes of peace and war. (I have not searched for others, but there are probably many more such organizations.)

The psychological qualities and attitudes that will be necessary for the achievement of world peace are:

- willingness to be satisfied with the borders of one's country in exchange for guarantees of peace
- having a neutral if not positive expectation of the citizens of other countries (not fearfulness of others in general)
- a wish that citizens of other countries can have good lives
- skepticism about any leaders' attempts to create hatred of others and all other justifications for aggression against other countries

For enduring peace, it may be necessary for all countries to join together to either invest in poorer countries so they can create decent lives for their citizens or to redistribute wealth so that the citizens in all countries have at least a decent life. This will not be equal incomes or wealth, since we still must honor individual effort and determination to make things better, but it is unacceptable to have significant numbers of citizens of the world die of starvation and disease.

I will treat other countries with respect and courtesy, while standing up for equal treatment for the U.S. I will propose and organize a treaty organization for world peace, by which all signatories promise to militarily support any member country that is attacked by another country (member or non-member). If any major countries sign onto this, it should be sufficient to control the inclinations of aggressive dictators to take from or take over other countries. We in the U.S. do not wish to take from other countries, so to belong to this treaty organization is not to give up any of our nation's sovereignty

Other Opinions

Human groups have always warred and taken from each other, and it is foolish to pretend that we can stop it. We should just stay the strongest, so no one will mess with us.

BEING NUMBER ONE

A background issue in considering how to conduct our foreign relations is the fact that the rest of the world is catching up to us in power and productivity. The U.S. has had an unusual position in the world since World War II in having an economic head start on other nations for being the major influence in the world politically and militarily. This has been good for all nations, generally, as the U.S. is not aiming for control or dominance—just happy to be in that position of number one. China is now in a position to challenge us for number one, and no amount of effort on our part will put this off forever. China can match us in research and development and has more manpower than we do, so *the best course for us is to remain very strong so that China is deterred from attacking us, even while we accept that the position of number one is going to be shared.* If China gets over its current need to gain respect in the world, then diplomacy should be able to make this sharing possible, since we can and do mutually benefit each other already in terms of trade. *I will treat China (and all other countries) with the same courtesy and respect and will expect good treatment of us by them.*

Other Opinions

The U.S. is slated by God to be number one, since we are the most righteous, so some way or other, we will remain number one. In addition, we are smarter and stronger than the people of other countries, so there is nothing to worry about.

WORKING WITH OTHER COUNTRIES

As the countries of the world become more interconnected and as human activity on the globe increases to the point of sometimes actually threatening our species' existence on the planet, solving these worldwide problems requires working together with other countries. Climate change is an example of this. Whether or not you believe that human activity plays a large part in the current changes in climate, the problems still exist (rising temperatures, ozone layer changes that permit more deadly radiation to reach the surface of the earth, rising sea levels, more deadly storms), and the only way to do anything about these things on a meaningful scale takes global cooperation. U.S. citizens alone cannot change this tide. Pollution of the oceans and air is another such problem (e.g., plastic pollution that you are consuming right now as microparticles in your foods, even though you don't know about it).

Effective work on climate and pollution will cost every citizen (and every person around the globe) financially, and it may result in a slightly lower standard of living, since it will require us to use more costly processes to recycle, to make things without polluting, and to possibly consume less. As world resources are reduced by our use of oil and gas, we will have to make things with greater energy efficiency or not make as much.

Americans are used to having unlimited resources and opportunities, but this will change, which will mean adjusting to how things really are and not to how we wish them to be. So far, most politicians are not being frank with the voters about these issues but are pretending that they are not important (because "science" will always save us through its research and development). Scientific breakthroughs are not guaranteed and are unpredictable, and it is not prudent to act as if we can do whatever we want, with no consideration for our own future and that of our children.

The Trump administration set a bad example for the people by withdrawing from international work on worldwide issues, particularly because this allows other powers, such as China, to become more influential in the world. Mr. Trump deserves some credit for the NAFTA revision and the NATO financial support deficit, but it is also foolish not to participate in large-group trade treaties which could be advantageous to us (like the Pan-Pacific Partnership). Outside traders always get worse deals than insiders, and Mr. Trump liked being an outsider. *I will work toward useful agreements with other countries that will benefit all concerned and will have some hope of success with everyone's participation.*

Other Opinions
You can't trust any other nation. Sooner or later their interests will diverge from ours. Trying to stay out of foreign entanglements was and still is good advice. Military alliances may be valuable for the short-term, but solving global problems is just too big.

NATO

NATO has been one of the most productive alliances among nations in this and in the last century—dedicated as it is to preventing the subjugation of one nation by another. Mr. Putin's latest aggression in Ukraine demonstrates the importance of NATO for world peace, at least any peace that does not allow subjugation of one nation by another. *I will continue our nation's commitment to and support of NATO (but note the radical proposal under "Russia" just above).*

Other Opinions
NATO simply commits our nation to defend other nations that are distant and unimportant to our welfare. We should let them stand or fall on their own. We have oceans to defend us.

THIRD WORLD DEVELOPMENT

The United States has a direct interest in the economic development of poorer countries for two reasons. Those countries' citizens look enviously at our standard of living and wonder why we were lucky enough to be rich while they are poor. This envy will continue until the lives of the poorer citizens of the world have improved until some sense of fairness or satisfaction is felt. If their lives do not improve, they will be vulnerable to many sorts of political extremist invitations, which will increase instability across the globe. The second reason is that improvement in their standard of living will almost certainly lead to a decrease in their birth rate, and this will help in controlling world population and defending world resources. *I will support funding for major economic development projects in these countries, as that will both aid in the needed development and garner us better relations with them.* China has been helping with these projects for at least ten years (their Silk Road Project), and it has multiplied China's influence around the world despite their calculating policy of (I believe) expecting these countries to default on loans so that the Chinese can take over more of these countries' land and assets. We need to set a better example.

RUSSIA

Since the end of the Cold War, the U.S. has been pretty much ignoring Russia and gone ahead with its own push to democratize (Vietnam, Iraq) the world, but it not wise to ignore or downplay the largest country (in territory) in the world. We have also, in the Ukraine war, simply vilified Mr. Putin instead of acknowledging Russia's legitimate concerns over the growing presence of NATO right on Russia's border. The U.S. would not allow such things on its border (viz., the Cuba missile crisis and the Monroe Doctrine), but we are unwilling to understand another country having the same concerns.

I view Russia as a country with a long-standing inferiority complex, that has striven mightily for centuries to be accepted as an equal among the Western countries. They have a ways to go in terms of developing an educated and active citizenry that will stand up to wayward leaders, but there has been progress in this regard. The best thing we can do in regard to Russia is to invite them to join NATO. This sounds absurd initially, but think about it! Russia may wish to make itself some excuses to enjoy some of its former empire-glory, and we cannot allow them to exterminate Ukraine, but I do not believe that it has designs on exterminating the U.S. (as it did up to the 1980s or so), so why not make them "one of the boys" and exert our control in that way rather than automatically assuming a war stance? I am assuming that the U.S. has no real interest in exterminating Russia, so why are we so reluctant to believe that the same could be true of a former foe? *I will extend some understanding to Russia and begin changing the long-held view of never-ending hostilities with Russia, including treaties and alliances for Russia with NATO!*

Other Opinions
All nations that have great power always seek to eliminate other powerful nations. You can't change that. It's in our genes.

UKRAINE

The Russian aggression in Ukraine is completely unjustified. Ukraine is not run by Nazis, and resistance by Ukrainians to Russia taking over their country is self-defense and not a threat to Russian society. The West has no designs to take over or obliterate Russia. The longer the war goes on, the lower Russia falls in the eyes of the world (including among the countries that publicly support Russia).

I will support the U.S. ensuring Ukrainian freedom by supplying funds and war materiel, for as long as it takes, sufficient to enable Ukraine to effectively prevent take-over by Russia. If we do not do this, Putin will be emboldened to do the same again (probably one or more of the Baltic countries). It is not clear yet whether it will be practicable for Ukraine to keep all of its eastern territory. If both sides run out of manpower, all sides may decide to let the people living there vote on whether to join Russia or stay with Ukraine. (It is a nasty ploy by Russia to infiltrate its citizens into the territories of other countries and then claim that since Russians are a majority (or an oppressed minority), Russia should take control of that territory.) *I will also reassure Russia that the U.S. has no designs on it!*

Other Opinions
We should let those countries fight it out without our interference. They are so far away that they are no threat to us. We have no alliances or cultural ties to Ukraine, so why raise our national debt by paying for their war?

We wouldn't like Canada to Mexico to join Russia, so we can understand a little bit of why Russia fears Ukraine joining NATO (even though NATO would never aggress against a non-member state). Our own Monroe Doctrine, which eventually forced Russia out of Cuba, is similar to

Russia's attempts to keep neighbor countries from joining NATO. If it's fair for us, why isn't it fair for them?

CHINA

After centuries of China, a truly ancient civilization, being humbled and used economically by Western countries (including the U.S.), China is asserting that it is just as good as everybody else and trying to prove this by expansionism (Tibet, Taiwan) and military build-up. China and the Chinese deserve to be left alone and to feel good about themselves, just as every other country is so entitled, as long as they do not aggress against other countries. Unfortunately the Chinese have a history of thinking of themselves as superior to other societies, and this may be reflected in their current assertiveness. Despite the bellicose talk by the Chinese Communist Party, I doubt that ordinary Chinese citizens want wars or conflict any more than ordinary Americans do. The problem, once again, is in our leaders and their drives to power. This does not justify China's underhanded methods, such as stealing trade secrets and other economic information, but we need to approach our relations with China by being scrupulously fair, and this will be my approach. Of course, we must also be strong enough militarily to prevent any actual aggression toward us by China. *I will approach China in a friendly way, hoping for cooperation, but I will also enforce our demands for fairness and for non-aggression.* Perhaps we should impose the exact same controls on Chinese companies operating in the U.S. as China does on our companies operating in China and see how they like it!

Other Opinions
China wants to dominate the world, and we must stand up to them every day. They are Communists and can never be trusted. We must be stronger than them. Our ancestors were right to be always suspicious of Chinese immigrants.

ISRAEL

I am completely willing to guarantee the borders and safety of Israel from all attacks, but it is my opinion that the Israeli government could tomorrow, even unilaterally, divest themselves of some of the occupied territories and accept the formation of an independent Palestinian state. I fault them for not doing this because they could do it without threat to Israel's existence. I understand that there is much fear within Israel about their safety and much reluctance to have a Palestinian state next door, but with U.S. guarantees against all aggression, I believe that they would serve the cause of world peace by accepting the establishment of that Palestinian state and allowing it to happen. This does not even require pre-agreement on what is to be done about Jerusalem, which can be worked out later. The establishment of a Palestinian state will take much of the energy to destroy Israel away from those militants who now dedicate their lives to destroying Israel.

There are those within Israel who believe that Israel is chosen by God to rule the world and who therefore aim to take over adjoining territories as much as possible (such as all of the West Bank). This attitude will not serve Israel well in the long run. All peoples have the human right to choose their own governments. Israel has already aggressed enough to take what it has now, and that aggression may be grudgingly acceptable by the rest of the world due to what happened to Jews in the Holocaust, but further aggression should not be acceptable. Israel has no right either to claim that it deserves to have the same boundaries that it did under Roman rule, just as no other country can justify taking over territories that is had decades or centuries ago just because it had them back then (such as China in Tibet).

Let's also be very clear about the difference between criticizing Israel and anti-Semitism. They are not at all the same. Any thinking person can legitimately criticize short-sighted or even racist Israeli attitudes and policies while at the same time being highly supportive of Israel's right to exist as a homeland for Jews and highly committed to defending that right. It is unfortunate that Israel came into existence through taking someone else's land, but the situation of Jews in the world in the preceding centuries gives some justification for us now for leaving things the way they are.

Other Opinions

The U.S. has always supported Zionism and Israel and must always do so in the future. Any break in that support, even small criticisms, is seen by Israel's enemies as giving hope that they can obliterate Israel in the future if they just wait long enough, so we should not waver in the least.

TAIWAN

China is determined to incorporate Taiwan back into greater China, which would be a catastrophic loss of freedom for the Taiwanese and a moral blackeye for the U.S. if we do not act to defend Taiwan's freedom.

(Taiwan's current government stems from those in China who opposed Communism and were forced to flee to Taiwan when the Communists took over.) Unfortunately, the relative distance to Taiwan from China and the U.S. makes it very difficult for the U.S. to marshal its forces there. *I will try everything we can think of on the diplomatic side to keep Taiwan independent and will help to arm it,* but sadly I do not think there will be enough Congressional support for us to actually go to war with China over Taiwan. The alternative would be to promise serious harm to China if China does take over Taiwan, and this could lead to all-out war (which is another reason to keep up our war materiel and readiness). We do not have the same empathic connection with Taiwan that we do with Israel, which leads us to be much more willing to risk a larger war to defend Israel than to defend Taiwan.

Other Opinions
- Taiwan is not strategically important to the U.S., so naturally we will give it up rather than go to all-out war.
- If we give up Taiwan, we can kiss the western Pacific goodbye, which will lead to considerable reputational and economic losses for the U.S.

AFGHANISTAN

Our intervention in Afghanistan did accomplish the main goal—to remove Afghanistan as a location where Al-Quaeda could grow, but our nation-building effort failed because we underestimated the persistence of the Taliban, the necessarily slow process of changing the local culture, and the loyalty of Afghanis to Islam (of the Taliban variety), while we overestimated the attractiveness of our way of life to Afghanis. We would have been better off cleaning out Al-Quaeda and then keeping that status through air and missile strikes rather than trying to create what was going to be, in effect, a new culture and country. I'm all for supporting peoples around the globe in their efforts to achieve democratic independence, but only a tiny number of Afghanis were asking us to do what we did. The situation of women in Afghanistan certainly seems reprehensible to us, but culture change is slow, and we are loathe to accept that. *I will continue to press for Afghanis to have what are considered in the rest of the world as basic human rights, while not closing our eyes to the needs for humanitarian aid in that country.*

Other Opinions
- If we had used more of our resources for Afghanistan, we could have changed the country, even if that meant doing away with many more Afghanis who did not want to change.
- The moral failures of the Taliban are so egregious that we were morally obligated to stay until the country did change, even if that took another twenty years.

INTERFERENCE BY FOREIGN GOVERNMENTS: THE "RUSSIA INVESTIGATION"

Throughout recorded history, groups have attempted to influence each other to gain advantage, sometimes through communication or negotiation and sometimes through violence. The situation is no different today. We assume that every country has spies, just as we do, and our country has attempted to influence the elections of a number of other countries (most often in Latin America), though perhaps not through the internet's social media. Unless we are willing to give up trying to influence the elections of other countries, it is hypocritical of us to be so upset about what Russia has apparently done in our 2016 and 2020 elections. And, we should keep in mind that we don't have actual hard proof that the Russian government was involved, even if we can trace some of the interference to groups within Russia's borders. We have identified a pattern of communications and a pattern of purchases of social media ads and postings, but none of that connects necessarily with the Russian government. We can only say that we can't imagine how it could not be connected with the Russian government, but that is not the same as having proof. (It is convenient to jump on to believing that it was the Russian government, though, since as human beings we always want to have someone to blame.) Since election interference is illegal according to our laws, we have charged some Russians with illegal actions and levied sanctions on some Russians who seem to have been involved.

Even though many saw the Mueller investigation as aimed primarily at Mr. Trump, the investigation was centrally about whether Americans of *either* party worked with the Russians (or anyone else) on the Russians' interference in our election of 2016. The other charges that might arise as a by-product of the Mueller investigation (lying under oath, illegal money transactions, etc.) are simply by-products and say nothing about the central concern. Any Americans who worked with the Russians (or any other foreign groups) to sway our elections should of course be prosecuted.

Other Opinions
The Mueller investigation is primarily political theater designed to damage in any way possible the Republican Party. It is impossible to believe that anyone, from Mueller on down, could have been unbiased.

SEEING THINGS FROM THE POINT OF VIEW OF OTHER COUNTRIES

Americans are not good at seeing things from the point of view of other countries. We tend to assume that anything we do must be right or OK, since we are "good," and any country that does things that are not in our best interest must be "bad." This is a highly oversimplified view of people, countries, and politics. If we give ourselves permission to do things that are not in the best interest of other countries, then we must, in fairness, give them the right to do things that are not in our best interest. We can dislike some of those actions and try to get other countries to change those actions, but we have no right to say that we are always right. it is important for our integrity as a country that we base our positions and actions on clear moral positions, and subverting other governments takes a good deal of moral discussion.

Since we do what is in our best interest, as we see it, if that harms other countries, then we should take that harm seriously and try to avoid it.

Since we do what is in our best interest, it is appropriate for other countries to fear us at times. There is no reason that they should always trust us, since they can count on us to do what is in our best interest even if it is not in theirs. It makes sense for other countries to have their own nuclear weapons, for example, since they can't ultimately count on us. We think, and most other countries think, that the best thing we can do to prevent nuclear destruction is to prevent other countries from getting them, and I tend to agree with this general position, but we have no moral right to condemn them for getting nuclear weapons, since we don't give up our nuclear weapons. In fact, *as President I would maintain an adequate nuclear arsenal, while continuing to try to get all countries to reduce their numbers of nuclear weapons through treaties.*

Other Opinions
- Of course we are an exceptional country, chosen by God to support democracy and Christianity. We err when we forget these central duties and pursue our own worldly ends. War, coercion, and decep-

tion on our part are justified because we have God's mandate to change the world.
- People are so selfish that no one and no country can ever be trusted, so it doesn't matter if we do things fairly. It's dog-eat-dog out there, and we need to survive.

WARS

War comes naturally to humans, since it can be crucial to survival of the group, but in modern times it can have horrendous consequences for millions of people, which makes it very important to control and minimize the occurrences of war. Contemplating war is complex, since we must try to understand the relationships between testosterone levels in young males, perception of threat (often incorrect), political manipulations of the public.

War can sometimes be necessary to pursue the survival of the nation, but war should be limited to this need. Aggression and wars for political or economic gain are immoral and should be avoided at all costs. Preemptive war is of dubious morality and should only be undertaken if there is convincing evidence that the feared attack will take place with a considerable certainty (90 percent?). Our Iraq war is an example of a preemptive war that did not have that 90 percent certainty, and deception was practiced by the government giving distorted evidence to citizens about the reasons for the war. The wars practiced historically by European nations in general to "take" territory throughout the world from indigenous societies for economic advantage (find gold; take resources back home; create a captive market for manufactured goods; etc.) are examples of unjustified economic wars (which falls these days under the general rubric of "colonialism").

Since our groups (tribe, nation, etc.) are absolutely essential to our survival, and since we hire people (a volunteer military) to fight for us, we have become individually willing to have the country go to war without considering the costs of war. This results in citizens signing up to go to war even when they don't know the reason for the war. If everyone watched a video about the horrors of war, we might be more willing to make the decision about going to war on the basis of probable outcomes rather than on the basis of instinct. Every war *will* result in some citizens (at least a fair number of soldiers) being maimed or killed, and their loved ones will suffer for these things as well. We should force ourselves to wisely contemplate the realities of war before we enter one, so that all elected officials, Congresspersons, and all other citizens are exposed to pictures of the material and human destruction that would occur, details about the monetary and human costs (depression, anxiety, disabilities, healthcare) of the war, and comments from veterans of wars about the experience of war. I am certain that this would temper the flare-up of "patriotism" and the urge to fight. *I will provide this exposure to the realities of war if ever we contemplate war.*

Citizens do have to be willing to risk their lives for the survival of the group in certain circumstances, but most wars these days are about economic and political advantage rather than about survival. We should also be financially responsible for each war. The practice of borrowing money to pay for a war (as was done with the Iraq war), which will be paid back by future generations, suggests to the citizenry that wars are cheap and that we don't have to pay for them, and this is utterly false. Every citizen from now on is paying for any monies that we "borrowed" to pay for these wars when they are active. *I will push for current payments for any military action we undertake, so citizens know how much war costs.*

The leaders we choose have an impact on going to war as well. You may think that you need the most bellicose candidate (the best fighter) as your President, but that will mean more wars. You can be sure that leaders who are aggressive and dominating will get you into more wars than leaders who are thoughtful and cooperative. (It *is* possible to find leaders, such as myself, who are both thoughtful and cooperative and resolute and determined to defend the country.) Of course, we need to keep our military strong, so as to defend ourselves and our allies as necessary, and if we don't keep ourselves strong, then China and Russia will no doubt hope to achieve military supremacy (which would not be in our best interest).

To bring a new concept to the table, I will propose a pact, to be entered into voluntarily by any and every country, by which each country pledges to join an active military intervention (together with all other pact members at the same time) against any country that aggresses against another country, whether or not that country is a member of the pact. If enough members join, especially the larger countries, then no single country will be able to stand against them and conduct a war of aggression. Any member country that does not contribute to such actions will be excluded from receiving that protection themselves. (One unlikely possibility is that before the pact gets too big, countries that want to be able to engage in wars of aggression may band together in the same way, thus creating a counterforce. This could result in a stalemate, but at least this process would identify clearly who wants to use aggression to take advantage of other countries, which would affect their diplomatic and economic relations around the world. Everyone would know that they cannot be trusted. The underlying principle would be supported—that defensive wars are acceptable but aggressive wars are not.) Since the U.S. has no wishes to take territory from other groups, this will not infringe on our sovereignty in any way (although it will require some expenditures that we might not otherwise have currently).

Other Opinions
Groups have always aggressed against other groups to further their interests. It's in our blood (which is why no country has laws against harming other countries). Any defensive pact may slow down wars, but it will not change our human nature—to want more and to take it when we can. Besides, wars are a good way to bring a country's people together!

GOVERNMENT SECRECY/COVERT OPERATIONS

Governments have always tried to gain advantage through spying and keeping secrets. One country doing this pushes others to do the same. The government that feels threatened by other countries keeping secrets will try to find out those secrets and may start keeping secrets themselves. This is similar to arms races, where no country wants to be behind in the race and all feel "forced" to build better arms themselves. Counties could, of course, just stop all this nonsense, but the instinct to be capable of taking what we want from another group (another country) and the natural distrust that groups have for any group that is "different" are strong enough to keep everyone in the race just to stay alive.

As part of this secrecy, the U.S. has run amok in terms of classifying information as "secret." The justification for keeping secrets is that the information is important to national security. This seems rational, but the temptation to keep better and better secrets has led us to classify more and more information as secret, and the ability to label something secret has been appropriated by many to classify as secret things that have almost nothing to do with national security but which the classifying party doesn't want the public to know about the classifying party. This has got to stop.

I will revise the criteria for "classified information" if needed. Nothing that by law could be legally discovered by the public should be classified, and information that is outdated and cannot be useful to adversary counties should be declassified. *I will also institute a process whereby all classified information must be registered as such in a central file as to its content. Quality control spot-checking will be conducted on a random basis, and any information improperly classified (i.e., for personal advantage or protection) will result in career disadvantage or criminal charges against the classifying party.* Classifying something but not registering it will be an offense as well. All classified information will be labeled as to who does the classifying, and no matter when such misbehavior is discovered, the classifying party will be sought out and appropriate punishment applied.

Other Opinions

We need our secrets, since we naturally want advantage over our adversaries. Any interference in this process will put us more at risk, and this danger makes it worthwhile to tolerate some misclassifying. They are doing it to us, so we have to do it to them.

HEALTH CARE

MEDICAL CARE

It has become clear from the experience of other nations that single-payer healthcare systems, with the government as the payer, are workable and produce better health outcomes (longer lives and fewer illnesses) and less expensive healthcare for citizens than a fee-for-service healthcare system like ours. *I will work to amend the Affordable Care Act and move it slowly toward a single-payer healthcare system along the lines of Medicare.* All qualified providers will be reimbursed, so citizens can stay with their current providers if they wish, and providers will be paid better than now under Medicaid and Medicare. We as citizens of the wealthiest country in the world should be able to ensure that every citizen receives the same level of good medical care.

The healthcare of this country's citizens cannot ever be provided both properly and efficiently by business, because the fundamental aims of large businesses are to make profits, and this will always be in conflict with providing the best possible medical care. The argument that consumers "decide" on total medical spending by how much service they seek is nullified by the factors that (1) consumers opt for all the emergency care needed with no thought of the cost, (2) consumers never know how much they will have to pay prior to a service because insurance does not make it clear to them, and (3) many consumers will always seek more care than they can pay for. Because of this ever increasing desire/demand, total medical costs will have to have some cap, but Medicare provides an example of having a set of approved and unapproved services that is acceptable to most consumers and keeps administrative costs low, so we know that it can be done.

It will never be the aim of my government to cut costs at the price of restricting services, but *citizens will have a say directly, via a yearly straw poll, regarding how much medical service they are willing to pay for through their* taxes, *(having been given information about what services would be paid for at different levels of taxes for medical care)*. It may be that we could have citizens choose a level of care (with its set of covered services and its monthly payment amounts). Citizens will always be able to purchase additional healthcare, outright and through private insurance, above and beyond any level provided in the single payer system.

It appears that healthcare costs will continue to rise faster than other prices, due to the fact that people will continue to want and insist on more and more care as we discover more and more useful procedures and medicines, so getting more voter input on how much they are willing to pay will help us to face this inflationary problem. We currently have our collective heads in the sand about how much care is necessary rather than just desirable and about how much we are willing to take away from our other spending (bigger TV's?) in order to have more healthcare.

Other Opinions

Any time government messes with things, they cost more, so we should avoid this by staying with our private pay/insurance system. Remember how patients were promised for the Affordable Care Act that they would be able to keep their preferred providers, which turned out to be an empty promise. Medicare has the feel about it that government will cut off more and more services to keep costs down, which is not fair to consumers.

COVID

The U.S. was ill prepared to cope with the Coronavirus19 pandemic, but our healthcare personnel and our public health people did their best to save those infected and to prevent as many deaths as possible through vaccines, lock-downs, and other measures. Unfortunately, CDC's public information tried to be too authoritative rather than acknowledging all along the uncertainty of their claims, since they were actually learning as they went. The disappointed reaction of many Americans to this led to suspicion and rejection of public health measures in general. *In future pandemics, which I believe will happen inevitably, I would direct CDC to be more honest about their claims, and I would seriously consider skipping lockdowns and allowing jobs and businesses to continue as possible, since it appears that countries (e.g., Sweden) that did not use lockdowns ended up with overall health results similar to those of the U.S. and other countries that used lockdowns. As long as the overall incidence and death rates stay in the one to two percent range in these pandemics, we may be better off by more directly allowing* citizens to choose their own risk levels (vaccination or not, staying home or not, avoiding social gathering or not) and then using the results of comparing those who chose lower risk with those who chose higher risk as educational material to allow everyone to re-evaluate their choice of risk level.

Citizens will have to face their responsibility not to infect their fellow citizens, if we all can agree that a certain disease is transmitted from individual to individual, and this could mean wearing a mask or limiting social contact. It would be immoral for citizens to assert their complete right not to do these things (like wear a mask in certain situations) just because they "don't want to" or because these measures are not as effective as we would like, and promoters of "freedom" in this regard will have to publicly acknowledge that they prefer their freedom, even if it means that more people will die.

ASSISTED SUICIDE

An individual killing himself/herself is suicide, with which we are all familiar, and there are many seeming justifications for wanting to die, such as impending death from another cause (usually a disease) or chronic pain that cannot be reduced by medicines. Since we no longer need to have as many people as possible in our communities, we might wonder why societies have such a feeling against suicide, making it in many jurisdictions, a crime in itself. Are we saying that the normal inclination of living beings to keep on living is not enough to keep most of us alive? Are we afraid that if we see someone else do it, then we are likely to do it ourselves? Are our lives really that bad?

Of course, some of the suicidal individual's loved ones may not want the person to die, but do they have a "right" to stop the person from dying? Do they take any responsibility for helping with the reasons why the person wants to die, or do they just wish to force the person to live? No one else can know better than the individual whether that person's wish to die is the better option, since we can't know the totality of anyone else's consciousness. We should therefore give the person's own wishes more weight than the wishes of anyone else (or society in general) for the person to go on living. I believe that the individual should have total and final control over whether to continue living or not.

When a person's reasons for wanting to die are more mundane, such as poverty, sadness, and hopelessness, then we can reasonably wish that these conditions could be alleviated in some way so that the person could go on with an acceptable life. Mental health treatment would be one option for this, though we are loathe to pay for making this reasonably available for everyone. We should make such counseling widely known by the public and encourage every person who wants to die to take advantage of this help before ending his/her life.

Consistent with my belief in the individual's right to die, it would be convenient if we had well-known chemicals for this purpose available through the internet for individual use (much as we have chemicals available for abortions), as long as the individual has had a session with a qualified mental health provider to discuss his/her wish to die. If the individual does not end his/her own life himself/herself, but instead seeks assistance (such as chemicals that will accomplish that purpose), I would be comfortable providing these chemicals, technical assistance in using them, and a location to use them (to ensure that they are not obtained for use on some other person).

As a compromise between the complete freedom to suicide and the fears that many have of allowing this freedom, I support society creating some requirements for providing help with this, to ensure that the individual's decision is well-considered and not impulsive and "unjustified." These checks could include being evaluated by two mental health professionals as to the sincerity and "well-thought-out-ness" of the wish to die and a waiting period of two months before the requested chemicals are provided. A person should be required to take the last step himself/herself, such as pushing the button to start the deadly chemical infusion. If the wish to die is sufficiently strong, it should be strong enough for the person to take the last action on his/her own. The downside of giving individuals more power to decide whether to live or die is that there will be some (hopefully only a few) instances in which the person's life would have gotten better if he/she had only waited a little longer, but I believe that having the "right" to decide will result in more good than the bad that results from not waiting longer to make that decision.

Other Opinions

No one in their right mind would kill themselves, so people should be hospitalized until they want to live again. To offer any assistance partially legitimizes the idea that is OK to kill oneself, so assistance should not be offered at all.

ABORTION

I believe, and I think a majority of Americans believe, that a collection of cells that have no human form is not appropriate for full legal protections as a "person." At some point in the gestation period, a human form can be perceived, though when that is probably varies quite a bit from perceiver to perceiver. (The claim by some that there is a heartbeat at six weeks is indefensible, as there may be some muscle contraction at that point, but there is no heart at that point.) The point at which the fairly complete human form is perceived is the point at which I personally would begin to think about legal protections of some sort. I am satisfied with the current common practice among states of allowing abortions up to some point at the choice of the woman bearing that fetus, often up to six months into the pregnancy (15 weeks seems reasonable), with exceptions even beyond that point for severe deformity, almost certain failure to thrive if born, and protection of the mother's health.

I personally do not think of the fetus as a full human being until birth. I also understand that many people think about this quite differently, often connected with their religious beliefs about the definition of a person. A particularly hypocritical aspect of the current battle over abortion is the anti-abortion strategy of not making women who seek or have abortions criminally responsible, while seeking prosecution of anyone who helps them. Women who seek and have abortions are in fact responsible morally, and if abortion is such a heinous crime, it is unbelievable not to prosecute the persons who are responsible!

I believe the best course to take for this issue is ongoing dialogue and finding the best compromises that we can at every point in time. The attitude of fighting until one side or the other "wins" is not the best way to proceed. We all must learn better to compromise, for the sake of all concerned, and to live with those compromises once made. *I will encourage this ongoing dialogue and all efforts to improve whatever compromises we come up with.*

Other Opinions

There can be no compromise on this issue. A human life exists from the moment of conception, and this life is sacred and must be protected as if it were a baby already born. To compromise would mean going against important religious beliefs, so we will fight on. It doesn't matter if we force other people to live the way we want, because we are right and they are wrong.

DRUGS

People use drugs to alter their internal states (their subjective experience of the moment), so the key question regarding alcohol and drug use (and abuse) is why people have such a need to change their subjective experience. Is life not OK without the drugs? Why not? Using a substance, most often alcohol, at the point each day when we transition from the intensity of work to a more relaxed "at-home" state has been with us for a long time and does not have to have negative consequences, but going beyond this—using drugs to escape from one's life—almost always has very serious negative consequences. We need, therefore, to examine why so many lives are so unpleasant as to need this artificial escape (hating one's job, hating one's family, hating oneself, feeling no closeness or support from others, seeing only lying and cheating around one, seeing no alternatives). Why isn't real life good enough?

Yes, some people seem to have a genetic predisposition or vulnerability to overuse, but drug abuse is not a disease but rather a condition, and we can alter our conditions if we have the insight to understand what can happen to us (and what is happening to us) and the determination to choose the best overall course of action for our lives. (A physical predisposition or vulnerability does not cause a person to take that first drink or use that first line of cocaine.) Avoiding overuse often rests on having the foresight to see how substance use/abuse leads so often to a worse life for abusers, and having the self-love to avoid those negative consequences. (Psychologically this requires making those negative future consequences as "real" in one's imagination as the immediate pleasure of escape or "feeling better" from using the substance, so one can fairly weigh them and decide on what is best for one.)

Here we see one of the unsolved psychological problems for our species—that we have no built-in limits for what is enough. If we pay attention to them, we have built-in limits for assuaging hunger and thirst, but we have no such built-in limits for how much is enough in terms of possessions, love, or security. Many times people feel driven to go so far in trying to feel secure and feel good about themselves that they harm themselves and/or others in so doing (taking more for themselves when others truly don't have enough for survival, kidding themselves that adulation or obedience are evidences of love, believing that having millions of dollars will make them happy). Many, many people would be happier in our society if they sought genuine and deep connections with others and the joys of benefiting others, while also having sufficient physical resources to maintain life.

I will support reality-based treatments for alcohol and drug abuse, without expending resources on people who may be in crisis but are not ready to actually change themselves. "Rehab" is too often just a period of respite while people gather themselves for the next period of drug use.

POLLUTION

For most of our human history, human beings have been able to use things in the environment without concern about the remains, waste products, or residual results. If a tribal band's campsite became too dirty, they moved the camp. If a factory produced poisonous waste, they dumped it in the river and let the people downstream worry about it. We have progressed somewhat in seeing the bigger picture, and as noted under "Climate Change," there are so many people now that our impact on fellow citizens is more visible. There has been some effort in our society to recycle product materials, but this has sunk to near nothing since it turned out that for many materials recycling had a cost great enough to keep it from being profitable.

It is past time for an attitude change in our society. It is time to view it as a practical (by law) and a moral requirement to use our waste for some other purpose, change our waste into something that is not harmful, or store it on our own property forever (which then could not be sold to anyone else because they would have to "own" that waste). This is similar to the notion held by many with regard to use of the forest or public campsites—use but don't leave any trace of yourself when you leave. It is the opposite of dumping your waste by the side of a highway (where everyone else dumps theirs, too). The concept is related to sustainability, in the sense that no activity should be carried on that could predictably lead to having to abandon a site or activity on that site.

Without this attitude change, we will continue to pollute our air and water and oceans until they poison us back in a widespread way. *It is a significant moral matter how we deal with waste products, since those waste products affect the lives of others.* It is no longer sufficient to tow waste out into the ocean a few miles and dump it or to pay another town or jurisdiction to dump your waste there, just as it has proven inadequate to bury radioactive waste deep in the salt layers below the Utah desert (since the barrels leaked). this shift will cost us all something—both producers and consumers, but without it, we will eventually kill ourselves and our culture. *I will support research into new ways to store, destroy, or transform waste.*

Other Opinions

You exaggerate. It's not that bad. There is still lots of land out there to dump it on, and there's lots of ocean left to pollute. It will cost our businesses too much to do what you ask. Those of us alive now will all be dead by the time this is really a problem, so let's just stay with how things are.

HOMELESSNESS

My understanding of the homeless situation, confirmed by people who actually work in the streets with the homeless, is that there are three major groups of those who are homeless—those who are circumstantially (and temporarily) homeless through loss of job, divorce, or domicile, those who are homeless mainly due to substance use and addiction, and those who are homeless mainly due to mental illness. (Many of these have both substance and mental problems.) Also, included in the latter two groups are some who prefer being homeless to having a permanent house or home, usually to avoid the daily grind and responsibilities of being a permanent part of any group.

Those who are circumstantially homeless need specific material help—a place to sleep, money for transportation to interview for a job (or maintain a job), proper clothes for job interviews, help finding possible jobs, perhaps moving expenses to another state where the right job is available, etc. We are reluctant to help these people because we are used to expecting everyone to do these things for themselves, without realizing how difficult it is to do these things while homeless. If you've lost your job, your clothes, and your car (and have no savings, like so many other Americans), how are you to find the cash to remedy any of this (particularly when we have trained Americans to spend all their money consuming, so that few have any savings to fall back on? Finding another job did not require so much of us in the past when things were simpler, but now everything is more complicated, and there is a much greater need for some fall-back ready cash. *My proposal for a "job for every person" above speaks to the help that I believe government should provide (which, by the way, in getting people back to being tax payers, benefits the rest of us directly).*

Those who are homeless due to addictions need help with addiction. There are public and private programs for this purpose but not enough of them—especially not enough of them for those without money. Also, this help takes time, and during that time, these people need a place to live and help in regularizing their lives and escaping the chaos that addictions have brought to them. *I will support development of additional helping facilities (recognizing at the same time that if a person really prefers substance use to normal life, we cannot help him or her).*

Those who are homeless due to mental illness have serious mental illness—psychoses, untreatable depression, or mania. We do not have enough public clinics to help these people, and most of the clinics now focus on maintenance (medications), while local governments give just enough cash help to survive but not thrive. We have given up on the seriously mentally ill (SPMI or SMI) becoming any more than peer-helpers to other mentally ill persons and do not expect them to become tax payers again. *I will support providing more treatment facilities for them (and providing government-supported jobs that can provide motivation for them to do more).*

Some believe that giving everyone a place to stay is the answer to all three of these types of homelessness, and certainly having a place to stay would be a great help to many homeless, but it does not in itself solve addiction or mental problems, and these will require perhaps a doubling of our professional helpers to assist with these problems. The greatest block to low-cost housing in our towns and cities is the refusal of other citizens to live near the currently homeless ("not-in-my-backyard"). Perhaps those neighborhoods who refuse to live next to recovering persons and homeless should pay a special tax to help maintain helping agencies.

Helping those who are homeless and do not want to have a home if it will mean participating as normal citizens in our society is a tougher problem—one that will not be solved by providing housing. Some simply don't want to work and prefer existing by scrounging, but many are unable to be normal citizens due to their life experiences, addictions, and/or mental illness. Helping these will require helping them to adjust to the many demands required of us "normal citizens" (such as following social rules and getting along with everyone around them).

An additional concern to keep in mind is that as our businesses move toward more automation and require increasing amounts of prior experience and expertise of hirees, the more homeless we will have. There are only so many starting-level, no-expertise job for this growing segment of society to fill.

I will press for establishing and maintaining the addiction and mental health treatment programs needed to actually make a difference and for funding for transitional housing for those needing the stability of housing help. This will be costly, but our response will show just how serious we are as a country about solving the problem.

Other Opinions

People have to take care of themselves and must solve their own problems. If they can't or won't, then they will just have to survive on nothing, and if they turn to crime, we will put them in jail.

REFERENDA

I will use national referendums ("straw polls") on various major issues in Congress to provide clarity on how much citizens want certain things and are willing to pay for those things. (Remember, the government only has *your* money, unless it borrows it or prints its own, which will result in debt or inflation or both.) You will therefore have a say every year about government expenditures.

Using referenda will give a more comprehensive look at what "the American people" want, since what we see in the media is mostly the wishes of the more extreme left and more extreme right, and these extreme wishes are thought to determine primary elections and therefore to have an outsized influence on our governance.

Since we are overwhelmed already with polls, why do more—because how you pose the question determines the answer you get, which the pollsters never reveal to you. I want to ask the right questions.

I realize that all of the things I am proposing in this platform if done at the same time would increase the share of our incomes going to taxes, so feedback and these referenda are ways of putting the brakes on that spending, since the voters should have the loudest say in balancing their taxes and disposable income.

Other Opinions

It will be too confusing to do national straw polls, since we won't know who exactly is responding. Also, will they really know what they are responding to, since right now they won't understand the issues in any depth?

PSYCHOLOGICAL FUNCTIONING AND HEALTH

There are psychological principles that can help us to have good lives (to take adequate care of ourselves and have a sufficient amount of time in which we feel good about ourselves and our lives) and to have good human relations in our country. The amount of divisive hatred between our citizens is clear evidence that we need to improve how we treat others. Here is a summary of those principles. (You can find more in my books.)

Our desires and motives are key to understanding why we do things. All human beings around the globe have the same basic goals and motives in life:

> survival
> minimal or at least tolerable physical and emotional pain
> some times of feeling positive emotion, which can be achieved
>> mainly through –
>> feeling good about ourselves
>> feeling secure and not afraid
> sex and raising children
> satisfying relationships with at least some others and acceptance in
>> our groups (family,
> friends, town, nation)

Everything we do serves one or more of these goals.

Actually, we can narrow this down even further by fully realizing the key role that feeling secure (not fearful or insecure) and feeling valued play in our daily feelings and functioning. Not feeling valued makes us feel undeserving and pushed out of our necessary social connections. Everything we do every day is motivated by these desires to feel secure and valued. When you get a job, you are seeking not just money but also security, good feelings about yourself, fulfillment, and gratifying interactions with others. When you choose a church, you are seeking not just a joint worship opportunity but also security, feeling good about yourself, and social relations that you believe will help you with your other goals.

Knowing that we are the same in terms of our goals/motives in life gives us a basis for understanding and appreciating the nitty-gritty of others' lives and for feeling compassion for them (caring based on seeing their suffering with a wish for that suffering to be lessened). Developing our empathy skills helps us to appreciate the experience of others. It has been pretty well proven that satisfying connections with others is the number one psychological element in having good emotional and physical health. I believe that a life focusing on love, peace, cooperation, and reflection (for the purpose of understanding and guiding ourselves through life) gives us the best chance of fulfilling the goals above. For much more detail about this, including other choices for lifestyle, see my book *Live Wisely, Deeply, and Compassionately*!

While the above goals may not be in the conscious awareness of most people, three things that we are all conscious of, starting in childhood, are—

> wanting to be special to our parents (and later to others) (to keep their love and support)
> wanting things to be fair (so others are not benefited more than we are)
> needing to be included and basically accepted in all of our groups, especially the family (so that we can survive and fulfill our own goals)

When we think about adequate functioning in the world, there are four major areas of psychological functioning that enable successful goal-attainment in life.

(1) your relations with reality and truth (including the ability to adapt/change) (seeking and knowing the truth, to the best of your ability)
(2) your relations with yourself (self-esteem, self-respect, self-love, self-acceptance, self-responsibility, treating yourself well)
(3) your relations with others (not harming them, treating others well, learning from and loving others, finding needed support, stimulation, and love)
(4) your ability to manage your emotions (including finding some amounts of happiness/satisfaction/contentment/fulfillment)

The better an individual does in these areas, the better he or she will feel and function.

Human beings always do what they view as being in their best interest, even when they seem to be acting altruistically. It is desirable for human relations that we make as many of our behaviors as possible also to be of benefit to others and not just to ourselves. Often sharing and taking turns with others are the things that will benefit ourselves the most!

Human beings are constructed to function quite well in our environment, unless they have internal conflicts or issues that cripple their effectiveness.

Human beings are constructed to have adequate happiness, unless they have internal conflicts or issues that cripple their effectiveness or themselves create painful emotions

My own definition of emotional health is –

> having all of your capacities available for use in seeking achievement of your goals (and having few, if any, internal conflicts or "symptoms" that would interfere with use of your capacities in a "smooth", integrated way)(e.g., wanting to go to college but feeling unable to because your parents would think you were disloyal to the family to want to have a better life)
>
> and, having an adequately satisfying subjective state (your moment to moment emotional experience of life), including feeling some amounts of happiness and hope, and ultimately some amounts of satisfaction, contentment, fulfillment.

Behaviors that do the most damage to emotional health (impair unconflicted functioning, lead to more emotional pain and greater aggravation and worry) are—

> believing things that make you feel better rather than believing things that are true
> being afraid to think for yourself
> letting others define you as inferior or worthless and accepting this (usually in order to preserve those relationships)
> distorting your own self-image (thinking of yourself as defective, inferior) in order to maintain needed relationships
> not accepting yourself as you are
> not treating yourself with respect
> not loving yourself
> treating yourself badly

avoiding your emotions

taking status hierarchy position too seriously (as defining your worth and not just your position for the distribution of goods in society)

doing things that are not in your best interest (since this either makes you crazy or damages your self-esteem)

being dissatisfied with something without doing whatever you are willing to do about it and then accepting the result with good grace

being afraid of others

being afraid to feel good in relationships

believing that you can get more in life by taking advantage of others than you can by attending to their feelings and cooperating with them

believing that you can get more in life by using force and power with others than you can by attending to their feelings and cooperating with them

isolating yourself from others

blaming others for what should be your own responsibility, including your own emotions

trying to get others to change instead of (1) accepting them and (2) taking responsibility for your own feelings and decisions

In order to have healthy self-esteem (to feel good about yourself), you need –

a healthy and positive view of yourself

being basically accepting of yourself (including determining your own humane and reasonable standards for yourself)

treating yourself with respect

loving yourself

a feeling of agency and the satisfaction of taking decent care of yourself and your loved ones (feeling satisfactorily successful and effective)

treating yourself well

having basic respect, courtesy, and acceptance from others

Form and move toward goals that will make you as happy, satisfied, content, and fulfilled as possible. You don't need status to feel good about yourself. Taking good care of yourself and your loved ones, raising capable and responsible children, and contributing to our democracy by working and by voting knowledgeably and communicating with your representatives are more than enough to justify feeling that you have had a successful life.

As a person, no one is "better than" you, and you are not "better than" anyone else

Our obsession with buying and consumption leads us to believe falsely that one who has more is "better than" others.

People benefit from being active, since this creates a feeling of adequacy and "agency" (being able to affect one's life positively). Instead of just watching screens (big ones or tiny ones) every night and all weekend, we will feel better about ourselves if we choose action (joining a local baseball team, playing lawn bowling or shuffleboard, joining a quilting club, setting up your own hiking plan, helping a food bank, etc.).

It is foolish to seek a perfect life or regret not having a perfect life, because, given our limitations and our existential position, no life or person is perfect, and we always have some blocks to goal attainment and some moments of unsatisfying emotional state!

The key to good human relations is to treat others as if they had worth—with basic respect, courtesy, and acceptance.

Difference is always threatening to people, so learning to tolerate difference (different views, beliefs, customs) is necessary for smooth, positive relations.

We must strongly encourage tolerance, basic respect, and basic acceptance of every citizen by every other citizen. We all belong here, and we are all in the same boat regarding the quality of our lives and our existence as a group. Our inherent human tendency to create status differences works against this, and we must learn and believe that rich people, entertainers, and the popular are not better than anyone else.

Everyone needs the positive feelings of taking good care of himself or herself, as well as of those dependent on him or her and of contributing to the overall welfare of the nation. This is why *everyone* should have a job, or some other contributory function (even the wealthy and disabled), as well as some variety of options for doing this.

Everyone deserves basic respect and acceptance, because everyone has basic value just for being human and alive. Each of us must believe in this basic value and must insist on the principle that no one is inherently "better than" anyone else. We do not need to feel better than anyone else to feel good about ourselves, and we should not allow others to do this to us without protest. We would not be better people or more worthy of respect if we had more money, but our obsession with buying and consumption leads us to falsely believe that these make us more worthy. It would be far better for us to value people for their contributions to the lives of others than to value them for their wealth or fame. Our emphasis on individualism has value in terms of supporting the sense of worthiness that we need as individuals, but it is keeping us from getting the satisfactions that we need from supporting and helping our fellow human beings.

I will speak to the psychological needs of all of us and support education and programs that enhance our well-being, including good self-esteem and healthy relationships with others.

I will also highlight the respect and admiration due to people who take good care of themselves and contribute to the lives of others, as parents, community members, and citizens of our nation.

Other Opinions

Mental Health is a bunch of bunk. People should man up and fly right! Put them in jail if we have to. Feeling sorry for victims is not helpful. Besides, we can't pay for all that therapy, which is rarely curative anyway!

NATIONAL DEFENSE
(Including Non-Military National Defense)

A strong military is essential at all times to protect this country from direct attack, and *I will ensure that our military is strong.* I wish more of our tax tmonies could go to helping our own citizens, but the fact there are many countries with leaders who would like to benefit from our demise or defeat means that we must be strong enough that that strength deters all attack. Technological progress is key to maintaining this deterrence.

Military means are not sufficient, though, to change any hatred by others toward our country. These hatreds must be investigated and understood and intercultural means undertaken to alter them and to make peaceful and mutually beneficial coexistence possible among all people. *I will establish an office or department that will have as its mission the understanding, in depth, of our impact on other peoples and nations and to recommend methods for improving those relationships.*

Other Opinions
Arms races are unwinnable, and more and more destructive capacity will ensure that some day, those arms will be used. It's not much to look forward to.

Another View—No other groups or countries are really trustworthy, so keeping "fortress America" the strongest in the world is absolutely our number one priority.

JUSTICE SYSTEM ISSUES

LAW AND ORDER

An organized society needs laws and methods of enforcing laws, and the police are the first line of enforcement. Theirs is a difficult task, since they must interpret behavior that they observe and must decide whether to introduce the observed person into a justice system that has some pitfalls and injustices of its own. Nonetheless we must have a justice system, and we can only try to make it the best that we can make it. *I am not in favor of any sort of "defunding" of police, since proponents of this and of changing enforcement completely into persuasion must then allow law breakers with more power to defy arrest I am in favor of changing the behavior of police to be unfailingly courteous and respectful to the public, including those who may have broken the law, and to use deadly force more sparingly than they currently do.*

I believe that the law should be enforced at all times as it stands. The "nine-miles-per-hour-over the speed-limit-is-OK" ruse weakens the whole idea that laws should be obeyed. There should be no exceptions to the laws for public officials and famous persons or for members of your own family! Rioters (as in our inner cities in response to supposed abuse by police) should be prevented from rioting and looting and not be let to run riot without control as occurred (shamefully) a few years ago on this country.

The laws are what we have agreed to through our elected representatives, and we all agree (simply by being citizens) that we will follow these laws. If a law is patently unfair, then citizens should protest and elect other representatives to change the law. District attorneys need some discretion in utilizing their employees, but by and large, only lack of staff can justify not enforcing some specific laws. If a law needs change, then change it. If our representatives refuse to change it, then it must be enforced.

In the course of a person's involvement in the justice system, the he/she/they should be treated at all times with respect and courtesy. If a person needs restraint in order to cooperate with the procedures, then restraint should be applied, but it should not be accompanied by verbal or physical abuse. We want all persons to follow the law, but we don't require them to be nice persons, so verbal and physical abuse aimed at making them act as nice persons is beside the point. The equal treatment that the accused gets in the courtroom should be the same as what he or she gets in the jail and everywhere else in the system. This will take a change of attitude on the part of justice system employees who now display our society's ambivalence about whether the accused it truly considered innocent until proven guilty and whether punishment is for the purpose of causing pain or to rehabilitate. *I will press for changing attitudes to actually treating people as if they were innocent all the way from arrest to conviction and changing attitudes from punishment by means of pain to punishment as a time for rehabilitation.*

PUNISHMENT OR REHABILITATION?

A key problem in our justice system arrangements is our deep ambivalence about the purpose of jail time—is it punishment or an opportunity to change an inmate so that he/she doesn't offend further upon release? Ideally we want jail to serve both purposes. Punishment as vengeance is so deep in our make-up that it can't be eradicated, so we will always be applying some pain, if only through incarceration. We see the prevailing attitudes of citizens in the courtroom when those affected by a crime usually demand greater punishment than the offender gets, but for all our sakes incarceration should also be a deterrent to further crime. (A few citizens report their forgiveness for offenders during trial, which is an attitude that would lead us to put much more into rehabilitation.) Our ambivalence about this causes us to treat prisoners in a disrespectful and contemptuous manner (intended as both punishment and deterrent), which, because it attacks a person' basic personhood, almost guarantees that it will push most prisoners into even more of a criminal identity than they had before. Not getting a supportive attitude from jail staff, prisoners turn to the other inmates for support and acceptance (like joining a gang for protection), and hence we reduce recidivism even less than we wish to because in jail, prisoners learn how to be better criminals rather than how to refrain from offending again. I believe that many people in jail would like to get away from further criminality.

If we really want to reduce recidivism, we must give a prisoner some encouragement, and we know that people respond to what is expected of them. If we treat someone with respect and courtesy, as if he/she were worthy of that treatment, then he/she is pushed to act as if he/she were worthy of such good treatment, and he/she will wish for more of that kind of treatment and so will think more about not offending again than if we treat him/her with condemnation and contempt. There are supportive rehabilitation programs in a few of our prisons now—that treat people as if they were already out of the criminal identity and that provide them with tools (often including job-preparation as well as religious or psychological counseling) for living a crime-free life, but more prisons don't adopt them because of our anger at offenders and our wish to punish them personally while in jail by causing them pain (by the attitudes that we take) and not just with incarceration per se (which is society's formal definition of punishment). I think it is more productive to change people for the better while in jail rather than punish them with personal contempt on the part of jailors, and *I will push for funding support for rehabilitation programs (programs that aim to rehabilitate, by giving people better identities to live up to as well as practical training and information about how to live a crime-free kind of life.*

Other Opinions

Criminals don't change, so you can forget about rehabilitation. We can never trust them again.

BAIL AND A SPEEDY TRIAL

The length of time between entering jail and being tried in our country is an absolute injustice – an insult to citizens who are "presumed innocent until proven guilty," and a blot on our national reputation. Only in the lowest level cases, in magistrate courts, like speeding, does trial take place in a speedy manner, as required by our Constitution. Of course, an accused should have good legal representation, including time to plan a trial strategy, but the ready issuance of continuances (delays) for one reason or another undermines any hope we have of later rehabilitation in most cases in which the accused stays in jail. Making cash bail more reasonable could help this situation somewhat. *I will promote legislation to require more speedy trials and require judges to carry out trials within specified time frames, except in unusual extenuating circumstances.* This may require doubling the number of our courtrooms and judges, which will take time but must be done. Footing the bill will challenge us to show how we really feel about having a just system!

Cash bail needs some changes. The purpose of bail is to guarantee attendance at a subsequent trial, but it ends up being another way of punishing people since if they cannot pay the bail, they spend more time in jail, quite often acquiring knowledge and attitudes that make them more likely to reoffend. I don't want people who are quite likely to reoffend let out, with or without bail, and I think that the likelihood of reoffense should be the main consideration regarding whether to require bail, rather than ability to pay. *I will look into this issue more deeply before announcing possible actions.*

Other Opinions

People who are accused are usually guilty, so it doesn't matter if they get a little additional punishment waiting for trial. Our need for vengeance requires that we have trials, so we cannot let people skip bail and disappear. And we certainly don't want to pay for more courts in this country. We want to make it awful to get involved with the justice system, so more people will try harder to stay out of it.

THE DEATH PENALTY

We think that a penalty of death for a crime is the ultimate punishment, reserved for the worst crimes. Many people, though, oppose the death penalty and think that this level of punishment should never be used. I think that for many prisoners, a life sentence without the possibility of parole is actually a worse punishment than death. Even serving a sentence of twenty or thirty years would for many be worse than death. *I personally think that society should have the capability of using death as a penalty for certain crimes. Additionally, I think that since an individual should have total and final say over his/her life (except for court sentences, of course), prisoners should be allowed to request their own (painless) deaths while in prison, whether or not they have been sentenced to death.*

I also think that the length of time it takes to actually carry out a death penalty is ridiculous. Appeal attempts (and their continuances) that are really used to put off the time of death, rather than having any possibility of justifying a retrial, should not be allowed. The squabbles over whether a method of carrying out a death sentence is "cruel and unusual punishment" are also rather silly. We know full well about chemical means of causing painless sleep and eventual death, and we should use them, if we are to have a death penalty at all. This might mean a lengthier process waiting for the drugs to take effect, while the body slowly dies, but it would not be "cruel" or "unusual." *I will research and inform state attorneys-general of these chemical means.*

Other Opinions
Life is always preferable to death, so people will always choose life if they can have it. This is why abolishing the death penalty is better. Even an entire life in prison is better than the alternative. This justifies stringing out the death penalty process forever, if that's what it takes.

OUR ADVERSARIAL SYSTEM

While our adversarial approach to trials may encourage attorneys to give the accused a reasonably good defense (in order to "win" against the opposing attorney), it also does damage to our concerns about truth. We empower attorneys to present false claims to juries (i.e, to lie), which I personally do not like, since it encourages an attitude on the part of the public that doing something wrong is OK if you can get away with it. In our society we have a strange love-hate affair with lawbreaking, admiring or being envious of successful criminals and being generally unwilling to own up to our own behavior and instead routinely pleading "not guilty" and hoping that the prosecution won't be able to prove the case sufficiently. *An adversarial system is not the only way to seek justice, and I would like to see us discuss an alternative.*

Other Opinions
Fighting is the American way, so it is natural for us to set lawyers up to fight each other, and everybody wants to escape punishment even when we are guilty. The system is working satisfactorily, so don't mess with it.

GUNS AND MASS SHOOTINGS

Greater restrictions on guns (banning assault rifles and large capacity magazines, requiring more background checks and registrations, red-flag laws, etc.) would help somewhat to reduce gun shootings and mass shootings, but guns will still be available and are so embedded in the psyches and fantasies (cowboys, heroes) of Americans that it is not feasible to restrict gun use and ownership to really eliminate the problem. This stalemate has prevailed for decades, so it is time to do something differeent. We should recognize that 99 percent of gun owners are never going to kill anyone, and hunting and sport users can shoot with essentially no danger to anyone else.

We could justifiably make it illegal (for a lifetime) for a person who has used a gun in the commission of a crime to again own a gun, but we can get more total benefit from a campaign to attend to needs of the majority of people who do mass shootings—citizens who are alienated and despondent, whether at work, in their families, or on their own. These people are rarely truly "mentally ill" or "crazy" but feel so isolated and/or rejected by everyone that they have no hope of getting the nourishing human contact that we all need to be happy and healthy. Such a campaign could convince society to treat those people better, and all of us can make an effort to recognize and accept them. Society should provide more counselors specifically trained to contact, connect with, and help these persons find healthy roles in society. These counselors should be stationed in hospitals, schools, social service offices, and community centers (though, given cost considerations, counselors already in these places will probably end up doing double duty by having this added to their specific jobs). These counselors do not need additional training, since they are already familiar with the emotional issues involved. They simply need direction to watch out for such individuals and proactively offer positive contact. *I will lead the way in educating our whole society about these needs and in organizing an effort to help.*

Each of us can contribute to this effort, by noticing the people that are alienated and disheartened and offering them a little something. (Believe me, they are all around you in all kinds of environments.) The American tendency is to let people be as isolated as they want to be (our rugged individualism), so we will have to overcome this and learn to be comfortable with at least some minimal efforts to help caringly. (In my opinion, everyone in our total group—our society—deserves acceptance and inclusion in that society—meaning a positive attitude toward them by others and a meaningful role for them in the work of the total group.) We can say hello or ask about obvious problems of the person who is struggling to relate to others ("I imagine that most people just look the other way or are afraid to meet you." "It looks like you have a hard time feeling comfortable around other people." "It looks like being around others makes you anxious."). The individual will probably shy away from these initial comments, but you can expect that and either pursue the issue at that time or patiently wait to build up some comfort with you for the individual through repeated positive or neutral contact (like when you see them every day on your route to work). You don't have to offer anything specific or material to such persons—just your acceptance, with a positive attitude. If we don't move to help these people feel more OK about themselves and about being a part of society, then we risk their reacting with a mass shooting, to express their anger and to get back at those whom they believe have ignored them.

People in this subjectively hopeless condition are afraid of what they expect will be the negative reactions of others to them, and they usually develop off-putting maneuvers to protect themselves (like expecting rejection and then acting in ways that almost guarantee rejection, to prove that they were right to shy away in the first place). They crave acceptance and warmth but may be slow to trust it. You need not take their rejection moves personally. Just know that you have the great advantage of being more comfortable than they feel, which means that you have had more acceptance and warmth in your life than they have had in theirs. If each of us could empathically understand their dilemma, we could do a little bit, costing nothing, to help. (It's another matter to go further than befriending such a person. Some people will wish to help materially or in another supportive role, like advising or advocating for the other person, but this can in some instances result in difficult entanglement, and only those who can tolerate this and persevere should get involved in that way.)

Other Opinions
People should take care of themselves, or they will just become dependent. If they are so dysfunctional that they can't take care of themselves, they should be in jail or in a hospital (or homeless—it's their own fault).

POLICE BRUTALITY

We have a problem with persons being injured in their encounters with police, although the frequency of these injuries is probably lower than it seems to be when we watch the news. Some of these are caused by policepersons who are simply overly aggressive by nature, and these should be removed from the force (and not hired in the first place). Many of these unfortunate occurrences are the result of the dilemma that police have in following their rules of engagement. The problem is that police are supposed to be in control, no matter what. So, they cannot just let people run away, and in some instances they must use physical force to keep people from running away (from "resisting arrest"). Sometimes this force is excessive (greater than in actually necessary) and sometimes, if the person continues to resist, it results in serious injury or death. We can appreciate the necessity of using force when necessary, but police need some leeway regarding our expectations that they will always be "in control" if we are to reduce these injuries and deaths.

The police need some new methods to stifle resistance (a big net?, a more effective taser?) and explicit permission in some instances to allow a person to run away. Do we really want to have police shoot people in the back while running away? Maybe in some instances police could pursue reasonably but assume that the person will be caught sooner or later, so that they don't become so angry toward the person who is escaping. In some cities, car pursuits are already being called off when there is danger to the public.

Another training issue with respect to control is how to approach people. In most instances police approach politely, but in some instances, police try to do the "shock and awe" thing and overwhelm resistance before it starts by being overly aggressive (like these no-knock invasions of a home, and particularly the Memphis incident in 1-23 in which the driver was hauled physically out of his car with little verbal prelude). Police need specification of how and when to be aggressive. In my opinion it is better to have a few people escape than it is to have more suspect deaths.

The control issue is also present when police encounter persons who seem mentally ill or under the influence of substances and are therefore not responding to police commands. In almost all of these incidents, injury/death could be prevented simply with patience, but police feeling that they must establish their control are prompted by this imperative to escalate force so that they can appear to have control. Allowing police to take their time with these persons or utilizing mental health personnel would help.

The incidents of police shooting someone they thought had a weapon and was trying to use it against them can be reduced also, with clearer instruction for police, such as to wait until the individual actually makes a move with a weapon. Waving a knife around is not an aggressive move but a defensive move. Shooting someone because they seemed to be trying to pull something out of their pants is not acceptable—not until the weapon is clearly seen and is being aimed at police. This may result in a few more police deaths, but it will save quite a few citizen lives. Being a policeman will always be dangerous, and police need to feel that they can protect themselves, but all risk cannot be avoided, especially when protecting police lives endangers citizen lives.

Something that gets lost in the sensationalism of our news reports is that almost all of the people killed by police would not have been killed if they had not resisted arrest. Talking back or insisting that one has not done anything wrong often lead to physical altercations. Refusing to get out of the car often leads to physical altercations. We know that many Black families, for instance, have "the talk" with their kids about how not to resist arrest, but we continue to see suspects challenge and resist police, whether that is out of anger or fear, and this often gets them injured or killed. Perhaps we need a campaign to publicly coach citizens not to resist, even when they are uncomfortable or fearful, while also guaranteeing them fair and respectful treatment in return.

I will push for an expectation that police will treat everyone with respect and courtesy and for more clear rules of engagement for police, including waiting to actually be threatened rather than just "feeling like" they are threatened, and including insistence on approaching people softly first. "Qualified immunity" that is used to prevent legal action against police for injury or death needs itself to be qualified so that unreasonable action can be punished.

Other Opinions

You don't know what it's like to be in a dangerous encounter like police are. It is difficult to act thoughtfully in those circumstances, and we can't expect police to. It's unfortunate that this results in some citizen deaths, but it is their fault for resisting arrest.

THE ECONOMY

GLOBALIZATION OF THE ECONOMY

As the economies of various countries move toward greater interaction and even integration (more trade), countries with lower standards of living will have wage advantages over those with higher standards of living, and there will also be more specialization of production (all items will tend to be produced by the countries with the lowest production costs for those items). This means that no country will make everything it needs any more, unless it isolates its economy from this global specialization (like having only exports and no imports, a condition that can only exist to a limited extent). Citizens of the U.S., for example may like paying lower prices for those items produced overseas at lower costs (like in China or at Walmart), but our society then pays the price of many U.S. workers losing jobs because another country can make their former products more cheaply. We can't have it both ways. This imbalance will continue until wages in the countries with lower standards of living increase enough that those countries no longer have a marked advantage in producing the products in question. Citizens in countries with higher standards of living will experience a lowering standard of living during this process (not just the U.S. but all developed countries), as their wages stagnate while other countries are producing their former products. This process of adjustment will take several decades, until all the workers in the world have roughly the same wages.

In the meantime, some workers in the U.S. will be out of work. If they wanted to, citizens of the U.S. could buy only made-in-America products, but the success of Walmart suggests that our citizens will not so restrict themselves for the sake of their fellow citizens who are out of work. Tariffs are tempting but will simply make some goods more expensive for U.S. citizens. Mr. Trump was right to insist on fair trade practices by all countries, but any protections of industries here will result in higher prices for U.S. citizens on these products. We could, as a country, decide to produce certain products ourselves even though they cost more, because we want to ensure employment for certain workers or because we don't want to be dependent on other countries for some items, like steel, computer chips, and medicines. We could make tariffs on these products so high that Americans would buy American, recognizing at the same time the higher costs to Americans of doing this. It's a value choice.

There are many advantages for us in participating in the global economy (lower prices, more things available), but the negative impact on certain citizens of the expansion of global trade should not be minimized. The nation (and their former employers, if the jobs were lost through the employer moving production overseas) should provide adequate assistance to all displaced workers to enable them to work again, including job training, job finding, and moving expenses, if necessary, plus six months of salary beyond termination. Former employers should pay for some part of this. I will move toward legislation to remedy this problem. (Note that the justification for this is that today's jobs are more and more specialized, and it has become quite difficult for people to find reemployment in which they can use skills from their former employment. Because of this, employers should have to weigh the advantages of moving work overseas against the costs that they will incur from having to help former employees resume their careers. This is part of their responsibility to society at large—a "cost of doing business." This is also the justification for having job-finding offices sponsored by the federal government in every town (see below).)

Other Opinions

A global economy will result in greater overall wealth. It's too bad that some workers and some countries suffer in the process, but eventually all will benefit.

INCOME INEQUALITY

While wealth allows people to be more comfortable in life, having great economic disparities among the people of a nation is destructive to democratic societies. People instinctively will tolerate only so much wealth disparity (because every member of a group wants basic respect, and in our society being in poverty gets no respect), and capitalism inevitably will operate to keep on increasing wealth disparities unless some catastrophe or war occurs to cause a reset. People in a group always desire some equality in the distribution of resources, and while they will tolerate some differences (usually based on the status hierarchy of the group), they will rebel if some have excess wealth and some not enough to survive or have a decent life (as compared to others in the same society).

Wealth beyond that which provides security and comfort has little point (beyond ego inflation). Fair and compassionate means must be found to restrict the gap between the poorest and richest in society, whether that is by straight out income redistribution or changing the tax code to keep disposable income for the rich below some specified level. (Republicans insist that if they have more income, the wealthy will "create" more jobs, but they never check to see if that actually happens. We should, therefore, give rich people a reward for every job created, not give them a tax break at no cost to them with no proof that they are benefiting society.) *I will seek policies that will ensure income sufficient for a minimum level of quality of life for all (at this point, $45,000 for a family of four?, $35,000 for a single person?), and I will seek to keep a large (perhaps fifty percent), thriving "middle class" in existence.* This will add tax costs for people earning more than these amounts, but it will also ease the moral unease and moral corruption that we have currently from allowing unnecessary suffering for many in our society.

Even if this proposal for a minimum income is not adopted, I will press for minimum wage requirements *in all jobs* that would enable recipients to have a "decent life." It must be done, one way or the other.

Other Opinions

Competition in an economy, just as in evolution, results in the stronger benefiting more and therefore in an even stronger economy. The poor will always be with us, the Bible says. We shouldn't let anyone actually starve, but we would be reversing evolution to do more than that.

CAPITALISM

Capitalism (defined as an economic system with markets of private capital available for investment, along with private ownership of economic assets) has produced the best results for human beings in terms of wealth, but capitalism has no "heart" with regard to distribution of that wealth among citizens, which promotes a "dog-eat-dog" and "take care of only #1" mentality in society. Human societies do not tolerate happily inequalities of wealth that are greater than a certain degree (unfortunately defined only in citizens' emotions), which has led historically to revolutions in which the richer citizens are persecuted and there is a great upheaval of wealth redistribution.

In order to preserve order in society, we should attend to the inequality issue and "tweak" our capitalism in such a way to ensure that all citizens have a decent way of life compared to all other citizens. This does not mean dollar equality, since it must still be possible for effort and vision to pay off for individuals in greater wealth. *I think that the best compromise is to have government supplement wages for the lowest earners to guarantee a certain floor level of income, and I will pursue this legislatively.* This level would be determined by a government-citizen panel according to the costs of houses, TV's, food, etc. This supplement would be funded by businesses and taxpayers, in a mix determined by Congress. Businesses who supplied their workers with higher wages would pay a smaller amount of this supplement. Persons receiving this supplement would be required to work, utilizing the "jobs for all citizens" and "a living wage for a decent life" sections below. I realize that this is a major change in how we conceptualize the relations between business and society, but for the sake of fairness and to avoid eventual rebellion, this step must be taken.

Other Opinions

Fighting over available riches is the human way. If people don't want to work hard, then they should be poor. It's their own fault. And, such a revolution could never happen here, because we're too rich already. Forget this soft-hearted bullshit.

JOBS FOR ALL AND WAGES FOR A DECENT LIFE

(See the chapter above for "JOBS FOR ALL AND WAGES FOR A DECENT LIFE.")

UNIONS

Unions should represent worker wage and benefit interests in discussions and negotiations with management. Since in publicly owned companies, management is always under pressure from outside (boards of directors, stockholders) to make maximum profits, they will always underpay workers as much as possible. We call this a "free market," but when workers don't have other options and pay is not sufficient to have a decent life, then eventually there will be a rebellion and the system will be changed by force. The people with money say that this could never happen here, but it will (and if it does, it will be the fault of owners and management for not sharing income appropriately).

Companies that try hard to give workers decent wages and benefits (enough to have a decent life) have few labor problems and have more worker loyalty, but unfortunately unions are necessary to counterbalance the profit interests of management in most companies. Of course, management doesn't want to be restricted by worker needs, but in order to have a system that we all can feel good about, we need a balance of the interests of owners and workers. *I will support having strong unions but will insist to both sides that they work together and meet the needs of both without the necessity of frequent strikes. I will speak publicly against unions that insist on worker income that will drive a company out of business. I will impose fair government settlements if management and workers are unable or unwilling to find the best possible compromise.*

Other Opinions

Unions impede economic growth and therefore impede economic improvement for all citizens. This improvement would be greater if done by "the market" rather than by unions. Workers are not capable of policing their leadership, which leads to a great deal of corruption and lack of effectiveness.

PRIVATIZING/CONTRACTING OUT

Capitalism has produced greater total wealth for societies than other economic systems, but private enterprise is ill-suited to do the best job possible in some areas that affect all citizens. Personal greed does not produce the best healthcare, educational system, or utilities systems, for example, and capitalism must be adjusted to ensure that citizens' needs are met in these and other regards. The predominant motivation of people providing healthcare, education, and public utilities must be good service to the people and not personal gain. (Of course, these "public utilities" must live within their budgets, as determined by government and the people.) Private contractors are free to sell their companies or stop their services any time they wish, which is not conducive to the public good if they are the only providers of such services. Similarly, private enterprise cannot be trusted to make long-term adjustments in services and products in a timely manner, since profit may not always be present or predictable (such as the need for a transition from oil to other energy sources that do not degrade the environment).

Other Opinions
Privatizing can save money for taxpayers, since private concerns don't have to give workers benefits or adequate pay for your so-called "decent life." Most citizens would prefer this to using the more costly and regulated government services.

SOCIALISM

"Socialism" has become a bad word used by politicians to vilify other politicians and to rally conservative voters. In these pejorative references, "socialism" is applied to everything that the government does for its citizens, like healthcare and providing compensation for child care for working parents. It will be better for all of us to focus on what we want government to do for us (and what we don't want it to do) and decide for ourselves on the life we want as a people as we go along, without the distraction of labels (conservative, liberal, socialist, communist). (Socialism is properly understood as the state owning the means of production, but the term has been so corrupted that it is now applied whenever the people together pay for a government service through taxes and then receive those services "for free," most commonly education, retirement, and healthcare.)

Thus, the only decision facing our nation about something that we recognize to be desirable for all is whether we wish to provide it to everyone in society through taxes or wish to have most people pay for such a service individually and have government, through taxes, make up the difference for those who cannot afford it. We must decide as citizens whether we want universal services of any particular type, regardless of whether anyone yells "socialism," because the only way universal services can occur (like universal education or the military) is for government at some level to fund and oversee them. Deciding to do something as a total group (like providing healthcare to all) is not socialism if it is the group's decision, and these decisions should be based on how best to solve the problem at hand. *I will encourage useful discussions of what benefits/services our citizens want to have universally and will support legislation to enable citizens to have those services (and, of course, pay for them through taxes and not individually).*

Other Opinions

People only work and make effort if they have to, so they must be forced to work through necessity. It's not fair for those who have the gumption to work and to seek a better life to have to pay for those who don't. Gradually, we'll come to a situation where no one wants to or thinks they have to work.

EDUCATION

EDUCATION

College has become a touchstone for whether a person is going to have a chance at having enough money for everything we generally want in life (nice house, nice car, comfortable retirement, good life for the children), and the cost of college education has grown enormously over the last fifty years. Universities have tended to become research centers with less focus on undergraduate education. The traditional seniority system for professors (tenure) has meant that more experienced professors cannot be required to do much work or to do work they dislike. Most teaching of undergraduates nowadays is done by teaching assistants or adjunct faculty (not even true employees of the college), rather than the professors who presumably have the best knowledge of the subject. There could be merit in redefining what colleges and universities are for, focusing more on undergraduate education, separating off grant-related research to research institutes, and abandoning the hope that putting all disciplines together in one institution (the university) as the only way to get cross-fertilization among disciplines. Our society may need another institution, not yet defined, to gather top scholars and thinkers together in a way that will better the thinking of all of them. *I will establish a series of conferences of educators and citizens to explore what types of educational programs and institutions our modern society needs.*

Another reason for the explosion of tuitions is that over the last thirty years, state governments have gradually decreased greatly their financial support for their state college/university systems (following the Reagan policy).

Our society has downplayed thinking, reading, and writing as life skills, instead focusing on the visual and oral and on the pursuit of immediate pleasures (for the sake of the economy). Most citizens exist in their small niche in society without ever thinking about why things are the way they are and without ever acting to make things better. One purpose of education should be to produce good citizens—those who treat their fellows well and who take seriously the responsibilities of citizens in a democracy. This should be done in required high school courses on citizenship and through the enlightenment of college students in required courses in philosophy and political science. *I will encourage state boards of education to again require citizenship information for secondary school students.*

Many colleges have abandoned their purpose of producing educated citizens and good citizens and have focused more and more on job preparation. Thus, we have lost higher education as a producer of better thinking citizens and focused more on the graduates of college making money. Many jobs that college graduates end up in do not require training at a college level to do well in those jobs (insurance salesmen, accountants, computer programmers, dancers, artists, etc.), and these persons could be better assisted in institutes for their various areas of function. Similarly, our society needs to be more appreciative of fixers and maintainers (plumbers, heating technicians, road fixers, etc.), and these again don't need college to do their jobs. College should not be a status symbol but a mark of advanced education and advanced thinking skills. In this sense, free four-year college for everyone is not appropriate, whereas training for career paths may be appropriate for government support. If college costs cannot be kept reasonable through other means, government should act to insure that the nation continues to have people who can think and plan at the highest levels, most likely through scholarships. *I will increase government support for trade and technical schools as appropriate alternatives to four-year college degrees.*

Our nation's public educational system serves not only to educate but also to meld us into one society. Unfortunately, primary and secondary education have become routinized, with insufficient progress in motivating children and providing varied learning opportunities. If charter schools become the societal standard, then they, too, will become routinized (bureaucracies do this no matter what). This is not desirable. Therefore, charter schools should only be for the purpose of demonstrating new teaching methods or school milieus that our public schools can (and should) then adopt. These new methods will no doubt cost more, and this will test our society's belief in the importance of education, as local districts will need more in taxes to pay for better education.

Teachers' unions are being blamed for the stultification of advances in learning methods, but we should also consider that youth today are not as motivated to learn what our schools teach as they were fifty years ago, which seems to me to be the result of increased media exposure to magical means of income together with a failure on the part of schools to give teenagers the hard facts of life—what it's really like to have a job, raise children, prepare for retirement, buy a house, et. Many teenagers think only of becoming rock stars or sports heroes when they grow up, which only a very few will ever achieve. In my opinion, making money through crude or useless self-exposure (like tik-tok, funny videos, and exposing everything about one's life in a vlog) gives no needed benefit to the country, even if a few young people are earning money at it.

There is currently concern on the part of some parents that their children are being taught things in school that are demeaning to those parents and that suggest to children that they should feel guilty for the problems of certain groups in society. They believe that this is occurring because educators are teaching "critical race theory" or other tenets of groups struggling for equality. I know of no secondary schools that actually teach "critical race theory,' but that does not change the fact that parents feel demeaned (with the help of certain politicians). I assume that if this happens it is an unfortunate outcome of teachers trying to convey the importance of viewing everyone as deserving of respect, rather than a deliberate attempt to demean anyone. *I will work to enhance the feelings of value and equality of all citizens without blaming anyone for anything, while still pointing out the destructive effects of prejudices and other beliefs that demean other citizens.*

There is a strong push in some states (notably Florida) to emphasize local control and give parents more say about what their children are exposed to in school. This is because there is no uniform viewpoint across the country on attitudes about race. What seems in Connecticut to be something everyone believes is actually not what lots of people in Florida believe, so there will inevitably be some differences in curriculum. The press has made much of the "don't say gay" bill in Florida, but if you look at the bill itself, most people could probably agree that it is not appropriate in third grade or under to actually teach about racial and gender issues, but this should not prevent teachers in those lower grades from treating everyone equally and demeaning no one based on race, gender, or gender inclination. The rejection in Florida of an Advanced Placement course in high school that deals with the racial issue in detail is probably coming basically from prejudice, but if you look at the Florida Education Department's requirements of schools, they do require the teaching of actual, complete history of race relations in our country and particularly in Florida. The point is that these new laws may not be as bad as the press coverage suggests.

Other Opinions
Removing the achievement of a college degree from lower middle and lower class children as a means of rising economically is unfair, and other avenues need to be opened up if college is to be only for "thinkers." Any alterations in our culture's beliefs and customs should be our decision and not imposed by "experts" and activists from outside.

EQUAL EDUCATION FOR ALL

There is some merit to having local control of education, but one of the frequent results of this is less money spent on educating poor and minority students than is spent on students from more affluent families (because people of a given class tend to live in the same neighborhood and go to the same schools). I will seek to require equal (per pupil) spending in this regard in every school district. Towns that discriminate in this way make a cruel joke out of education as a means of doing better in one's life and should be ashamed of themselves. On the other hand, parents of students in each public school may wish to contribute money to their own children's education (to augment what the schools can afford on their own budgets). *The best compromise here seems to me to be that such contributions can only be used for "frills" (extracurricular activities, nicer band instruments, the senior trip, etc.) and never for improving the actual education of their children, so that we can maintain truthfully that every child gets the same opportunity for actual education.* (Parents may of course pay for private schooling or seek charter schooling for their children.)

Other Opinions
School boards should have the power to decide school budgets, and this should be done in a color-blind manner.

NEWS AND ENTERTAINMENT MEDIA AS EDUCATION SOURCES

As noted above, an informed citizenry is essential to electing people who are best qualified to solve the nation's problems. Voting for the candidate that one "likes best" (or is the tallest or the richest or the most good looking) is no longer good enough, when the problems that need solution are now so diverse and complex. With people reading newspapers much less often (and reading less often in general), we have become to a much greater degree a nation of the visual and oral, and of course everything must make money. Mr. Trump has called the media the enemy, but they are simply self-centered businesses, busy making money by telling people what they want to hear (and trying—most of them—to also present the truth). Network TV news makes money but is woefully inadequate for educating citizens about any of the details regarding the nation's problems, serving to alert us to problems but not to educate us about them. The cable news channels (CNN, Fox News, MSNBC, etc.) lean liberal or conservative and present only one view, and since most viewers watch only one or the other (the one they "feel" most comfortable with), they get a one-sided view of issues. Opinion programs on cable news channels are geared to make people feel a certain way and do very little to educate. From the responses of persons on the cable news programs' roundtables, one can deduce a few valuable facts, but these discussions do not go into sufficient depth to reveal all of the pros and cons of specific proposals, let alone the background facts or understanding of the problems being solved.

As President, I will work to start a non-partisan TV source for in-depth learning about the nation's current problem issues and things citizens need to know, such as taxes, spending versus a balanced budget, how "the market" works, the Israeli-Palestinian conflict, nuclear proliferation, the national debt, economic globalization, education costs, climate change, etc. This source would employ researchers at government expense and would be scrupulously unbiased. It would include staff of both liberal and conservative persuasions. It would identify the positions of both conservatives and liberals on each issue, together with the pros and cons of those positions, and it would present the facts in enough depth that citizens could then intelligently question candidates for public office about what they intend to do. The presentations would be organized as education rather than entertainment. Media providers such as Comcast and Sony would include these programs in their programming packages sold to media deliverers such as DirecTV and Dish Network, because these would help fulfill their FCC obligations to provide a certain amount of education and public service announcements.

From all sides, there will be criticism of this new learning source. For-profit entities could do scrupulously unbiased programming if they wished to, but it would reduce their profits. They may claim that they are giving viewers what the viewers want, but what viewers want is apparently not sufficient to turn the tide away from superficial opinion to thorough rational assessment, which is needed to reduce the rancor in politics and the class conflicts in our society, as well as to produce better informed voters. People's feelings and uninformed opinions are important, but they are not an adequate base for managing our country. Feelings tell us what we need to attend to (in this case, important issues for the country), but opinion should be based on a thorough investigation of the available facts and the history of a problem.

Many will claim that there can be no such thing as unbiased reporting and education, but that should not be an excuse for airing only claims (opinions) that feel good but are not supported by evidence. (This applies at all levels, including many college professors.) It is unfortunate that problems these days are so complex that there are not enough reliable facts to reach unassailable conclusions, but to reach the best possible conclusions requires attending to the facts available and placing those in a context informed by expert opinion and history. To put it bluntly, it takes serious thinking, and we need to create a forum that encourages this serious thinking by more of our citizens. We do not want a class of "experts" at the top to be able to hold the country hostage because no one else thinks about things. If networks or other opinion sources need an education in how to do this serious thinking, I will be happy to help them to learn the basics.

Other Opinions

People are never going to learn enough to vote on the issues, so it is necessary to guide them through emotional appeals. And, you admitted that it is next to impossible to arrive at "unassailable" conclusions about our complex problems, so why try all this education?

STUDENT DEBT

Much has been made of the possibility of forgiving a portion of the debts that recent college students have acquired due to the high cost of college, the repayments for which are a serious drag for years on their spending once they are out of college. Two entities are at fault here. The first, in all likelihood, are the people (bank employees, college employees) who negotiated the loans in the first place, if they did not go into detail with the students about the costs of repayment (what it would actually be like), giving them the repayment amounts but also cautioning them about the amount of restriction that these repayments will place on their economic situations after college. Students and their parents who were not taking appropriate care in deciding whether these loans were appropriate for them also bear some responsibility.

We cannot simply forgive thousands of dollars in loans without sending a completely wrong message about citizens' responsibilities in financial matters. I would be in favor, though, of the government facilitating the alteration of repayment options such as consolidating loans and extending repayment periods as requested by the students. Don't forget—we are not going to tell the bank that made the loan to just eat the cost of cancellation. If there is loan forgiveness, the lenders are going to be paid off with your taxes. Another way to look at this is to ask whether individuals who support canceling this debt would be willing to contribute themselves to a fund to repay those loans (so that those willing to contribute would bear the cost rather than putting the cost on all taxpayers, as they propose). The government does not have its own money. Only taxpayers putting in their tax monies will create the means to cancel these debts.

Other Opinions

In taking out huge loans for college, students and parents were only following society's dictates about what it takes to get ahead, and it is unfair that their income after graduation is not high enough to allow repayment while getting on with life goals (buying a house, having children, etc.). In this sense it is everyone's fault (all of society) that this situation developed, and everyone should pay to correct it.

RACE AND IDENTITY

DIVERSITY AND DIFFERENCE

Differences among people (racial, religious, opinions, customs) are threatening and to some extent emotionally disturbing to all human beings, no matter how tolerant, and they are sources of conflict that can never be fully resolved. Human beings are instinctually afraid of those who are different (because not understanding them means that we cannot predict what they will do), and while that difference may be tolerated, especially in a country such as ours, it will never be as firm a basis for a polity as similarities in language, dress, and customs. We can consciously compensate for this innate fear and become able to live together with those whom we view as different (as long as they are not an overt threat), but this takes some psychic energy to maintain. Therefore, world peace is served by slow movement toward people having the same customs, language, and other factors that help people to understand and feel comfortable with each other, and this is why some degree of assimilation of immigrants is necessary to keep a society from splintering and falling apart. No one's culture or customs need be abandoned in total, but we must ultimately choose between having more sameness among people versus having endless conflict.

Liberals/progressives use appeals to the notion of equal rights to try to bring about greater acceptance and equality of opportunity, and this is useful, but it cannot eliminate the discomfort that we feel when we don't know others well enough to predict their behavior toward us. Of course, a good solution to this dilemma would be for us to get to know other individuals who are "different," so that we are reassured that they are just as decent and good people as we are!

Other Opinions

America has always been a mix of groups of people rubbing up against each other. It's too bad that this sometimes results in race riots and fisticuffs, but that is who we are. Let's give up trying to understand each other and just duke it out! To the winner belongs the spoils.

RACIAL/ETHNIC CONFLICT

Claims by some groups of people to be superior or better than other groups are destructive to the body politic of a democracy, since they seriously injure the self-esteem and motivation of the supposedly inferior groups and give the supposedly superior groups a false sense of value. *I will informally discourage all groups from claiming that they are "better than" others. I will encourage interactions of all citizens that create a sense of togetherness and being "in the same boat," since we need to work together in order to make this the best country that it can be. I will also seek to institute a requirement that all youth contribute a year of service to society—the Peace Corps, the Teacher Corps, or other public service organizations (or two years of military service, since that is probably the minimum that the military would need to train and use a recruit).* This will help young people to realize that there are people who have other worldviews but that they can work together with those people who are different to reach important goals as long as everyone accords each other basic value and treats others with respect and courtesy.

Other Opinions
Competition is the name of the game in our society, and groups will compete for value. No one actually wants equality, since everyone wants to believe that they are special.

BLACK LIVES MATTER

Of course Black lives matter, every bit as much as any other lives, and joining together to point this out and to point out continuing demeanment is highly appropriate. The Black Lives Matter movement is not out to put down whites but to claim an equal place in society. It's shameful for our country that they have to do this, but it seems to be necessary to cause some change to occur.

Other Opinions
No one is oppressing anyone else. There is no systematic racism in our country. There may still be some prejudiced people, but they will pass on soon. Let's be patient and let nature take its course.

IDENTITY POLITICS

All groups deserve to be proud of themselves, but identity politics is ultimately destructive to democracy, since it promotes difference and not togetherness. Differences are always to some degree threatening, even for those who try to understand others. When lower status groups first try to become equal, it is understandable that they emphasize pride in themselves as they are (even though they are different), but *I will work to make every group actually feel equal, which will make group competition for being worthwhile irrelevant.*

Seeking apologies and/or reparations from "oppressors" may give an illusion of progress, but when history has moved on, I think that reparations will be shown to have been net non-productive and to have only encouraged more accusations and blaming. Giving reparations will bring out much anger and hatred from those who are equally disadvantaged but not Black. The logical end result of paying people for social harm would be to compensate everyone every year for their amount of disadvantage (race?, poor quality schools?, lack of local jobs?, lower IQ?) the previous year, and that is not what we want, is it? Fighting over who is more oppressed may promote banding together with others who agree with one, but it also emphasizes the low self-esteem of all those individuals, which is not where we want to end up. The rights of all must be equal, but that is gained by actually feeling equal and not by distinguishing oneself from others, unless that distinction is not harmful to others. Also, giving people money as compensation may be useful for the recipients in the very short term, but it also serves as an excuse for everyone else not to change their prejudices!

Other Opinions
How can anyone feel good about themselves when others view them negatively? Those others are not going to give up their status without a fight, so oppressed groups have to claim that their views and beliefs are just as legitimate as those of others, and this means conflict. As President, it looks like you will try to avoid conflict too much. Conflict energizes people to better themselves.

AFFIRMATIVE ACTION

The effort to build middle class citizens from those who come from disadvantaged communities through what was known as affirmative action (reserving college slots for them to bring in disadvantaged persons) was an important public acknowledgement that background and family circumstances play a large role in whether or not a child can "move up" to a better life. (Ethnic background was the key concern here, but poverty would be just as good a reason as race to make these efforts.) Over the long haul, however, this sort of enforced advantage created complaints of unfairness. A similar complaint, in our courts now, claims that limits on the percentages of Asian students in college are unfair. *I believe that making additional (new) slots for the purpose of bringing more disadvantaged children to college is appropriate but that setting aside existing slots (thereby reducing opportunities for other groups) for that purpose alone is not appropriate. I further believe that at this point in time, college admissions should be color-blind and therefore that admissions panels do not need to know the ethnic background of any applicant for those general slots.* (Colleges can certainly restrict applications to only those from U.S. citizens if they wish.)

Other Opinions
Without special help, which can seem to some to be unfair, children from disadvantaged backgrounds will never be or become competitive in college admissions, thus guaranteeing even more of a class system in our society than we have now. You can't change this without this special help.

"WOKENESS" AND CANCEL CULTURE

The phenomenon of "wokeness" is currently a focus of contention for us. Basically those who are "woke" have been awakened to the problems of inequality in our society (racial, gender, and economic). The "woke" persons in the media are more educated, liberal, and better off economically, and they focus on the immorality (in their minds) of attitudes on the part of other Americans that promote or maintain inequalities. The backlash from their public criticism and demeanment of the "unwoke" has been resentment on the part of those other Americans about being told what to think and how to feel by these self-appointed warriors for equality or by the government and thinking that the demeanment dished out by the "woke" warriors is itself immoral and benighted.

The behavior of "woke" persons is somewhat foolish, since criticizing and putting down people will not change their minds and usually makes their resistance even stronger. It may cause them to stop publicly saying what they think, but it will have only a small effect on their actual thoughts, beliefs, and behavior. The "unwoke" who are criticized and demeaned betray by their resistance that they don't feel secure enough in their beliefs to simply dismiss the "woke" as a bunch of crazies.

An unfortunate by-product of wokeness is the tendency to create a mob and "cancel" offenders, usually involving social media. This has resulted in some publicity-shy employers firing accused workers inappropriately (certainly without due process). Untrue harmful criticism (claiming that something is true about a person that one does not know is true or could reasonably know is untrue) should be outlawed, and we should keep in mind that much that other people say is true is not in fact true. You cannot pass on as fact what someone else says if you yourself cannot confirm it. Slander and libel laws should be strictly enforced. You can say "I think that so and so did that...," but you cannot say "So and so did that..." if is it untrue or if you should reasonably have known that it was untrue.

Hopefully there are a large number of Americans who are concerned about the inequalities in our society but who work on it in their own ways, quietly, rather than publicly criticizing others. As you can see in this platform, *I will work diligently to make things in our society more equal racially, with respect to gender, and economically, and I will not be demeaning anyone in this process.*

Other Opinions
- The "Unwoke"—Don't tell us what to do or how to feel. We like what we think and feel just fine.
- The "Woke" – If you are not publicly correcting other people, individually and collectively, as needed, for their attitudes, then you don't really see the inequalities (and don't care about them).

RELIGION

RELIGION AND PUBLIC LIFE

Religion has for eons provided important orienting beliefs and information to human beings, who benefit through comforting ritual, answers to existential questions (why are we here?, where did we come from?, what are we supposed to do here?, what happens after we die?, etc.), guidelines for behavior, reassurance about risks and uncertainties, structure for customs (marriage, diet, etc.), and group support. On the other hand, religion has sometimes been the basis for wars and cruelty. (Note the Russian Orthodox church's current legitimization of the Russian invasion of Ukraine and the general tendency of a nation's churches to support its wars.)

In this country, we wish to allow the free exercise of all religions, but an individual's free exercise cannot include interference with or significant burden on persons of other faiths. Thus, we regulate the public expression of religious views, as in rallies, marches, or protests, when we set up rules for these events, such as not allowing incitement to violence. This does not prevent religious expression but prevents unnecessary burdening of or harm to other citizens. We also do not allow non-payment of taxes because someone disagrees with a few of the expenditures of federal monies on what they claim to be religious grounds.

I do not agree with business executives and religious groups who claim that paying for birth control or abortions through their institutions' health insurance plans violates their religious principles. Their integrity and their principles are not being denigrated by the fact that others engage in birth control. They are not asked to engage in those practices themselves, and paying for those services for women who wish to engage in them is not promoting those services to others if they are simply complying with Federal law. Following the law takes precedence here over their beliefs, since they are not expressing their beliefs at all by having their businesses (not themselves personally) paying for the services in question. This is not an issue of free speech, since spending money is not speech, just as donating to a political campaign is not speech. (The Supreme Court was in error there, in my opinion.)

I also do not agree with the claim that making a wedding cake with two gay people on the top is violating the baker's religious freedom. No one thinks that doing this says anything about the baker's own values, just as we would not assume that a driver delivering chairs for a gay wedding was endorsing gay marriage. The Supreme Court has just protected creative activity as protected speech, but that would still not allow refusal to simply copy what the customer wants the provider to say (on a cake, in a website). One solution might be to put a sign in the window of such businesses notifying the public of the services not provided to identified groups, but I doubt if such businesses would like to do that, since they would not want to notify potential customers who support gay rights of their stand. This is a difficult issue, and the country is feeling its way along to try make the best compromises possible. *I will seek to ensure that religious expression is protected, as long as it does not threaten or infringe on the rights of others.*

Many citizens are wary of Islam these days, because a very small minority of Muslims engage in violence against other Muslims and against believers from other faiths. I believe in keeping our facts straight. Islam does not have a central authority such as the Catholic Pope, so it is not possible to say definitively that "Islam teaches this" or "Islam teaches that" (since local religious leaders teach what they individually believe), but it is clear that even though the Koran has some passages urging violence in certain specified circumstances (e.g., protecting Muslims from violent attack), the vast majority of Muslims do not agree with using those passages in the Koran to justify violence in other circumstances. There are far more supposed Christians in this country who wish to overthrow the federal government than there are Muslims with this goal, so again, let's keep things in proper and accurate perspective.

Other Opinions

I shouldn't have to associate myself in any way with beliefs I don't share. I shouldn't have to live next to such believers or be on committees with them or sell them things in my store. I tolerate them, however, because we are a free country, so long as it doesn't make me look like I agree with them.

WHAT I BELIEVE

Candidates for President usually face the question "Do you believe in God?" during campaigns, so I will address that right now. I think that a loving and personal God, being omniscient, all-powerful, and perfect in Himself/Herself, can communicate with human beings if He/She wants to. Several individuals in Jewish and Christian history are reported to have been so contacted (Moses, Jesus). I have not yet been so contacted, so I am still waiting for this contact, which I believe would be unmistakable if it comes. I see no other certain evidence in this life that would allow me to "know" for certain that God exists, although many people interpret events and phenomena as giving that evidence (sunsets, babies, the feeling of awe). Knowing how willing human beings are to fool themselves with their interpretations and beliefs, I am not satisfied with these evidences, nor do I take at face value anything that self-appointed priests, ministers, and pastors tell me. I am open to this contact with God. In fact, I have been a part of Quaker meetings for several years, where the worship format is waiting in silence, together, attuned to possible intimations of such contact.

While I have been waiting for this contact, and since I think that a loving, personal God wishes us to succeed and be happy, I have worked hard at figuring out how such a God would want us to live. My conclusions are evident in this platform. I believe that we live best when we feel good about ourselves, use our talents to further our lives and the lives of others in the community, and have positive relations with others. Having positive relations with others entails treating them (all of them, at all times) with respect, courtesy, and compassion. My conclusions seem to me to be quite consistent with things that Jesus taught as reported in the New Testament (love your neighbor as yourself, be honest and responsible, try to be good people, forgive, be merciful, seek understanding, be pure in heart, and be peaceable and peacemaking (see in part the Bible, Matthew 5:3 12). I do my best to live by these injunctions and principles.

Other Opinions

You must think pretty highly of yourself if you think you merit contact by God! Human beings are weak sinners. Be satisfied with what you are. Make the most of what God has given us instead of insisting on your own criteria for how God should act.

WHAT WOULD JESUS DO?

This phrase, "What would Jesus do?", has importance for all Christians who aspire to be more like their Lord and Savior. If taken seriously, it calls on Christians not just to go to church on Sunday but also to pay attention to the Bible and their beliefs throughout the rest of the week. The key elements of Jesus' admonitions regarding everyday living are (1) to love God and (2) to love one's neighbor as one loves oneself. His teachings and parables also indicate that he believes that we should treat each other with compassion, understanding, honesty, responsibility, appropriate forgiveness, and with concern for others' suffering. He clearly valued love, peacefulness, and kindness.

I agree with all of these concepts, and I strive in my daily life to live this way and to treat others this way. Even though I am unsure about the existence of the paternalistic God most Christians believe in, I am positive and enthusiastic about all concepts that help us as human beings to have the best lives possible, and I think that Jesus' teachings are a good guide for this. I believe that all persons have an inherent value that makes them important to us. I try to always think of others as basic equals with myself. I do my best to put others' concerns and feelings on a par with mine in importance, so that I can treat them fairly and with love. I have great compassion for the suffering of others, and this is the main reason why I would like to be President. As a psychologist, my lifelong passion has been to understand others accurately and with compassion. I am carefully honest with others, especially when I know something that others could be harmed by if they are not aware of it. I am thoughtfully responsible in all my dealings with others. I do not hold grudges, and I do my best to maintain a positive and hopeful attitude toward every other person and the possibility of a positive relationship with him/her in the future. I try my best to live with love in my heart for everyone every day, and my concern for the suffering of our citizens leads me to seek peace and a more peaceful society (and politics!). I think that those who know me would attest to my being a basically kind person.

A VERY BRIEF SUMMARY OF MY PRIORITIES

We must restore a sense of equality and belonging among all our citizens. Each citizen should have equal impact in determining our country's laws and directions. No person is inherently any "better than" any other citizen, and notions of class and being "better than" others are destructive to our democracy.

We must restore a sense of comfortableness, peacefulness, and harmony within our society. This can be accomplished by accepting our basic equality (that no one is "better than" anyone else), treating all other persons with respect and courtesy, and at least to some degree caring about the welfare of each other. I will model this attitude of equality and acceptance. All disadvantaged groups, such as women, MAGA supporters, children, ethnic minorities, he disabled, and gender non-conforming citizens will be treated as equally well as non-disadvantaged citizens by all members of my administration.

There is such a thing as "truth" in the sense that we can work toward determining what is as close as we can get to truth. Everyone is entitled to his/her own opinions and beliefs but is not entitled to claim that his/her opinions and beliefs are true without some justification that others can understand. We should be tougher with those who claim to be making true statements with no justification, especially those who do this purposely to mislead other citizens.

Our two major political parties have too much power over our laws, since they allow their members to have only the parties' ideas and to vote as the party directs. We need all the good ideas we can get, and those should all be expressed so everyone can see. All Congresspersons should vote as they believe and not as the party directs. Parties should be prevented from punishing members who do not vote with the party.

Democracy is ideally a system of gathering the equally valuable input from all citizens and then fashioning the best solutions possible at the moment for each and every problem. Democracy should not be about who can "win" and force everyone else to do as they direct; it must be about making the best compromises possible on every issue. Our two-party system and our emphasis on winning make us enemies unnecessarily. I will work for effective and acceptable compromises for all of our problems.

Our taxes are not money being "taken" from us but are how we jointly pay for the government expenditures agreed to by us through our representatives in Congress. Taxes are not something to be avoided at all costs, and we should not idolize those who do best at avoiding paying their share. Everyone should contribute to the taxes that pay for our joint spending, even a small amount by those not currently paying any taxes. Citizens should not focus on whether taxes are too high but rather on what they want to include in our joint spending that is paid for by those taxes. Citizens can always elect other representatives if they think our joint spending is not being managed appropriately.

I propose that taxes each year should be based on and cover the spending approved by Congress the previous year. This will show you exactly how much your representatives are spending. This can eliminate government borrowing and allow us to pay down part of the scandalous national debt each year. I will also explore changing to a "flat tax" where everyone pays the same percentage (with the elimination of most current deductions). If the government wants to encourage certain behaviors (like installing solar panels), it should send citizens a check rather than reducing their taxes, since reducing their taxes makes us want to reduce our taxes in general when we should actually focus what we want to accomplish through government spending.

We do a poor job of electing the best qualified person to be President, since currently candidates try not to reveal very much about their true beliefs and intentions. The job of President is too important to be the popularity contest that it is today, where many voters vote for the best-looking candidate or the candidate they have seen most often in the news. We should always elect the person who is best qualified to actually do the job. Candidates should be required to reveal their intentions on a variety of key issues. (See my analysis of the job of President and the skills required in my campaign book (*A Compassionate and Moderate Political Platform for 2024*) and at www.livewiselydeeply.com under "government/politics" and then "presidential choice.")

People feel good about working when it contributes to the welfare of themselves and their families as well as the welfare of the country as a whole. We have too many people not working (homeless, disabled, not prepared for the current job market), partly because businesses want everyone to fit into the same limited model of an employee. I will propose a national system of job-finding and job-developing offices that will both match people to jobs and work with employers to create jobs appropriate for as many of the unemployed as possible, the wages for which will be paid for partly by businesses and partly through our taxes. This will be a net boost to the economy as well as to the emotional health of these workers.

We have many full-time jobs in our economy which do not pay enough to live on, leaving many unable to have their own places to live and unable to afford even a limited life in our economy. I will explore ways in which we can ensure that everyone who works receives at least enough in wages to have a "decent life" (the definition of this to be determined by Congress).

The effectiveness of our democracy depends on gathering the views and ideas of all citizens (and then finding the best compromise solution possible). Citizens should be able to discuss these ideas with each other, to broaden our views and to nurture a spirit of working together, but this is difficult for many who just want others to agree with their views. We can have useful, civil discussions about difficult issues by seeking to let others know about our views and why we think what we think, while learning about why others have the views that they do, instead of trying to convince others to change their views. I will model this mode of interaction myself and encourage this same tolerant and accepting attitude among all citizens.

The principles of good emotional health are not difficult to understand (basically, seeking to be happy through having adequate self-worth and an adequate sense of security, while valuing and not harming others). I will promote programs that support citizens' self-worth and security and help them understand what makes for good emotional health, and I will help society to help especially those who could end up trying mass shootings of their fellow citizens!

We must engage Congress in the essential job of revising our immigration policies and determining how many and which immigrants we want every year. We need some immigration in order to have enough workers in the future for our economy, and there are specific categories of workers that we need as well, such as seasonal farm workers and experts in science and technology. We must then spend the money to treat our immigrants humanely, including having enough immigration hearing officers at the border to hear every case within two weeks while those persons are waiting at the border in comfortable facilities to be either admitted or immediately deported. I am in favor of requiring every person admitted permanently to apply for citizenship within two years, since all differences between people arouse a certain amount of fear and since a certain amount of assimilation is necessary to avoid unwanted tension between groups of different backgrounds.

You can find more information about my positions on my campaign website ebbeforpresident.com (available in September, 2023). You can also explore my essays over the years on public affairs and morality at my first website www.livewiselydeeply.com. There will be opportunity on ebbeforpresident.com to donate to furthering the campaign ideas, if you are so inclined.

MOST IMPORTANTLY, DON'T FORGET TO VOTE! (write-in "Christopher Ebbe" if necessary).

FINAL WORD

I hope this look at what I believe about politics and about what is good for the country is helpful for better defining your own views and concerns. Of course, good decisions benefit from up to date information, so what I would do in office might be somewhat different from what is presented here if there is important new information at that time. For the good of the country, demand that all candidates be as open about themselves and who they will be and what they will do in office as possible, and press them for specifics! See my website (ebbeforpresident.com), Twitter, and Facebook for my blog comments (and opportunities to volunteer in my campaign Sept. 2023 to Oct. 2024!)

BIBLIOGRAPHY

Coleman, Peter. The Way Out—How To Overcome Toxic Polarization. Columbia Univ. Press, 2023.
Cohen, Geoffrey. Belonging: The Science of Creating and Bridging Divides. Norton, 2022.
Harcourt, Bernard. Cooperation: A Political, Economic, and Social Theory. Columbia Univ. Press.
Kornfield, Jack. The Art of Forgiveness, Lovingkindness, and Peace. Bantam Books, 2008.

APPENDIX A

Use this rating system to compare candidates.

(You can simply checkmark that the qualification is present, or you can use a simple rating scale (1, 2, or 3, with 3 the best) to help separate candidates.)

candidates
A   B   C

___ ___ ___ has the physical ability to persevere through an elected term

___ ___ ___ has ability to study and understand complex issues and systems

___ ___ ___ willing to learn from others and use others' knowledge to solve problems

___ ___ ___ has ability to predict outcomes of various courses of action

___ ___ ___ uses advisers who are competent and not just those who agree with him/her

___ ___ ___ can compromise on solutions/policies when doing so is demanded by the exigency of the situation and the impact on the public (rather than insisting on "winning" or achieving "wins" for extreme positions)

___ ___ ___ has the emotional strength to do the right thing rather than, in some cases, do what others want or would approve of

___ ___ ___ has the emotional strength to do what is best for the country even if it would act against his/her re-election

___ ___ ___ will collect only the amount of taxes that will pay for the financial commitments that Congress has made in the previous year.

___ ___ ___ has clear position on government borrowing and national debt, with anannounced plan for repayment (rather than a vague expectation that the economy will grow or that there will be more in tax revenues than Congress can spend!)

___ ___ ___ will not increase the national debt

___ ___ ___ will nominate judges for their judicial ability and fairness rather than for being liberal of conservative

___ ___ ___ has worthwhile ideas about reducing the influence of money (campaign contributions, advertising) on elections

___ ___ ___ will challenge political parties to give up power competition and do what is best for the country

___ ___ ___ will "level" with citizens as to who is preventing passage of needed legislation, even if it is his/her own party

___ ___ ___ will support getting legislation that is clear and specific enough to not need "interpretation" by the Supreme Court

___ ___ ___ carefully considers long-term consequences of all actions, not just short-term benefits

___ ___ ___ can see both (all) sides of every issue and addresses them in announcing his/her decisions

___ ___ ___ accepts that there is value in the considered view of every citizen

___ ___ ___ is respectful of all, even when disagreeing

___ ___ ___ has a keen understanding of people and their needs and feelings

___ ___ ___ has good judgment

___ ___ ___ has strong concern about the welfare of *all* citizens

___ ___ ___ will treat all citizens equally, rather than favor certain groups or favor those who have supported him/her

___ ___ ___ seeks office to serve and not primarily for fame or power

___ ___ ___ has strong speaking and writing skills

___ ___ ___ communicates effectively a vision for a better country and a better life

___ ___ ___ makes effort to inform citizens of intentions, particularly during decision-making processes

___ ___ ___ is honest and candid; tells the truth rather than hiding behind words, especially when the truth is personally embarrassing or will make some citizens mad

___ ___ ___ is responsible; takes care of business, no matter how difficult; does not blame or hide behind others to cover his mistakes

___ ___ ___ is trustworthy (can be trusted to reliably do the right thing)

___ ___ ___ is forthright enough to respond honestly to voters and co-workers, rather than hiding intentions and views

___ ___ ___ has integrity (is consistent, takes responsibility, and acts consistently with his/her values)

___ ___ ___ sets an appropriate and moral example for citizens

___ ___ ___ is committed to fair treatment of all and to not favoring those who are close or who support him; does not favor campaign contributors or lobbyists over others

___ ___ ___ tells citizens the negative effects of his/her positions, as well as the positive

___ ___ ___ does not promise things that he/she could never deliver

___ ___ ___ will "bring the nation together" by seeking what is best for all rather than favoring only some groups of citizens

___ ___ ___ has reasonable position supporting getting all citizens to vote (voter suppression? voter ID laws? early voting? non-partisan defining of voting precincts? protecting vote counts from hacking? improving accuracy of voter rolls?)

___ ___ ___ will act to reduce the effects of money on elections (limiting campaign contributions? reducing campaign period?)

___ ___ ___ respects and adheres to the Constitution's separation of powers between legislative, executive, and judicial branches of government, rather than belittling or trying to bypass the legislature or courts

___ ___ ___ seeks cooperation among nations rather than threatening and bullying them

___ ___ ___ has a vision of the sort of world order that will benefit other nations as well as the U.S.

___ ___ ___ will work with other countries to solve global problems (climate change, mutual defense, trade, human rights, nuclear threat)

___ ___ ___ will adhere to treaties and alliances as promised

___ ___ ___ has a fundamentally moral concept of appropriate government action and foreign policy

___ ___ ___ will keep the military up to date and effective

___ ___ ___ will seek a fair solution to the Israeli-Palestinian problem

___ ___ ___ can interact comfortably and effectively with those who are different from him/her

___ ___ ___ can speak inspiringly to citizens, calling them to be the best they can be

___ ___ ___ can cheerfully serve as a symbol of the country and of the government in formal and informal actions that give a good impression of the country and the citizens

___ ___ ___ will seek to reduce the wealth disparity in our country, by reasonable means

___ ___ ___ will act to help all wage earners to earn enough to live on and have a "decent" life

___ ___ ___ will act to help workers displaced by globalization to find employment (support from former employer and government? retraining? paying moving costs to relocate for jobs?)

___ ___ ___ will protect our free speech traditions rather than suppressing speech that upsets some citizens; will lead efforts to help citizens ferret out the truth

___ ___ ___ will encourage all, including candidates, politicians, and citizens, to adhere to the truth, rather than using speech for self-gain

___ ___ ___ has a cogent plan to assist homeless persons to re-enter the work force and/or accept help from programs of various levels of government

___ ___ ___ has a cogent and prudent plan to prepare the country for climate change (not too fast, not too slow; without disadvantaging workers in some industries more than others; without creating inappropriately high energy costs during transitioning to green energy)

___ ___ ___ will seek reasonable reform of immigration laws

___ ___ ___ has a cogent and fair plan to provide all citizens with access to a reasonable amount of healthcare

___ ___ ___ will act to reduce gun violence in the country (licensing of owners? background checks for *all* purchasers?)

___ ___ ___ will act to better define religious freedom (public expression? burden on other citizens? opting out of anything that one doesn't agree with?)

INDEX

Abortion   156
Acceptance among citizens   37, 46
Adversarial justice system   175
Affirmative action   199
Afghanistan   145
Amity among citizens   37
Autocracy   134

Bail/speedy trial   173
Balanced budget   80
Basic human psychological needs   17
Black lives matter   198
Borrowing   80

Campaign platform   9
Campaigns, presidential   133
Candidates, motives   130
Capitalism   183
Caring for others   38, 48, 53
Children   59
China   143
Civil discourse   99
Climate change   115
Competition   31
Compromise   31, 74, 75
Constitutional convention   127
Counting votes (methods)   131
Covid   154

Death penalty   174
Democracy vs. autocracy   34
Diversity and difference   197
Drugs   157

Economy   181
Education   189
Education, equal for all   192
Education, news and media as sources   192
Effect on society of the platform   10
Elections   83, 129
Elections, costs   134
Elections, security   133
Emotional health   163
Equality   18, 42

Fairness   24
Federalism (federal vs. states)   125
Feelings toward others   40, 42
Financial accountability   120
Foreign relations   137, 139, 147
Fossil fuels   116
Free speech   113

Gerrymandering   132
Globalization   181
Good government   17, 20
Guns   175

Healthcare   153
Homelessness   160
Honesty   23, 64

Identity politics   199
Immigration   109
Income inequality   182
Informed voters   30
Infrastructure   119
Integrity   25
Israel   143

Jesus   206
Jobs   91
Justice system issues   171

Law and order   171
Legislation, votes on all bills   124
Love   38, 48, 53
Lying   66

Marginalized or disadvantaged citizens   55
Mass shootings   175
Medical care   153
Men   58
Merit hiring by government   121
MeToo   57

National debt   80
National defense   169
National service   33
NATO   140
Non-gender-conforming citizens   60

Official language   127

Personal history and background of Christopher Ebbe   13
Police brutality   177

Political alliances   32
Pollution   159
Population   117
Pork   121
President, power of   22
President, choosing   83
President, job tasks   84
Privacy   114
Privatizing/contracting out   185
Psychological functioning   163

Race and identity   197
Racial and ethnic conflict   198
Rating presidential candidates   215
Referenda by citizens   162
Rehabilitation in prisons   172
Religion   203
Religion in public life   203
Religious beliefs of Christopher Ebbe   205
Respect   18
Responsibility   24
Russia   141
Russia Investigation   146

Secrets/covert operations   150
Senate representation of small states   124
Serving all citizens   28
Social media   67
Social security   119
Social status   18
Socialism   186
Speech, political   65
Student debt   194
Suicide, assisted   155
Supreme court   122

Taiwan   144
Taxes   77

Term limits   131
The Wall   112
Third world development   141
Treating others   44
Trump   135
Truth   63
Two-party system   69

U.S., status/predominance   138
Ukraine   142
Unfunded mandates   126
Unions   184
Unrelated amendments to legislation   123

Vote trading   32

Wages for a decent life   95
War   148
Welfare   98
What would Jesus do?   206
Wokeness/cancel culture   200
Women   56
World peace   137

(President\indexcampaignbk)

www.ingramcontent.com/pod-product-compliance
Lightning Source LLC
LaVergne TN
LVHW010202070526
838199LV00062B/4457